Detmar & Haskell Dialogue #5

C000115209

The Nature of the Political Left & Right

The Seven Philosophical Dictums of Politics and How They Determine the Behavior of the Left & Right, the Free Market, War & Peace, and the Rise & Fall of Empires & Corporations

---

CHRISTOPHER ANGLE

ISBN 979-8-9877707-0-2

Publisher: RITE Report Inc, 100 Research Dr., Unit 16, Stamford, CT 06906

Email: Detmar-Haskell@rite.report

Other Detmar & Haskell Dialogues in their chronological order by Christopher Angle:

The Nature of Aesthetics
The Nature of Ethics: Defining Ethics, Good & Evil
Truth and the Nature of Decisions
The Philosophical Equations of Economics

Table of Contents

Prologue..6

Chapter 1: Political Parties & the Origin of the Haves & the Have-Nots... 9

Chapter 2: The Dictums of the Haves...25

Chapter 3 - Control & Knowledge...70

Chapter 4 - Summary.. 88

Chapter 5 – The Philosophical Definition of Free Market Enterprise...105

Chapter 6: The Nature of Peace...117

Chapter 7: The Nature of Violence...123

Chapter 8: The Rise & Fall of Empires 147

Chapter 9: The Rise & Fall of Companies... 157

Chapter 10: Overview...160

Chapter 11: Goodness, Profit, & Aesthetics...............................177

The material herein and hereinafter will bear the influence of two teachers of the University of Michigan — Detmar Finke and Frank B. Livingstone.

Prologue

———•o◇o•———

There is a knock at the door of a professor of botany at the University of Michigan whose first name is Detmar. The Professor uses his first name because he always likes to converse with his students on a first-name basis. Detmar says in a strong voice, "Come in," and lo and behold, Haskell, a long-time conversant of the Professor, walks in.

Detmar says in a strong voice, "Come in," and lo and behold, Haskell, a long-time conversant of the Professor, walks in.

Haskell: Hello Professor; long time, no see!

Detmar: Yes! Haskell! Indeed! I'm so glad to see you again!

Author's Aside: The reason why these two are so happy to see each other is because they previously have had long conversations of philosophical import from which there were generated four works on aesthetics, ethics, truth & decision-making, and free-market economics, each book respectively defining the nature of these concepts. Haskell has received his Ph.D. in philosophy. But there's a special reason why he visits the office of the professor. It is that Professor Detmar has an excellent proclivity that is applicable to the discipline of philosophy. Detmar has the knack of being able to define almost any concept.

As Haskell has now a new interest in the nature of political philosophy, he's got some questions about various concepts that arise from his musings, and so he seeks out the Professor to help him clarify and unravel the various conundrums that have entered his mind. Haskell needs to resolve these matters because he wants to write another dialogue and this one would be what is transcribed here.

H. It really is great to see you, Professor!

D. And likewise! I have always loved our conversations. It is so interesting to dissect the various subjects that we cover. It gives me great pleasure.

H. Yes, Professor. As you know, I have used our conversations as the basis for the four books I have written; and today is no different as to the reason why I am here. It's another subject of great concern, and I might add of significant importance in the political theatre. So much is written and spoken about politics in the media, and yet, the abstractions in the polemics are almost never defined. It is in that regard that I have come here today. I would like to discuss the concepts in current media pertaining to the subjects of politics, war, and peace.

D. That sounds pretty interesting! But it's a wide array of subject matter.

H. Every day there's a dialectical tension in the media between the ideas of the Left and the Right. This contest of ideas is exhibited in all the editorials and the famous newspapers throughout the land and also in radio talk shows, podcasts, TV, books, and editorials, yet they all do not have an explanation of the very basic philosophical concepts that they use.

D. Well, that is a huge arena of ideas. There's so much to cover. What have you got in mind?

H. Well, actually it's not that huge. There are three areas of philosophical content that I would like to cover.

D. And these are?

H. As just mentioned, the three very basic areas of philosophical thought in the media are the political parties, war, and peace. What I would like to ask is: in the first instance, what is the nature of politics? Let me rephrase that: first, what is the nature of the political party? Where do they come from? Is there a nature? Where would one start if you were a political scientist looking to understand the nature of politics, war, or peace?

D. Interesting! This will be good!

Chapter 1: Political Parties & the Origin of the Haves & the Have-Nots

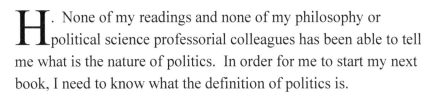

H. None of my readings and none of my philosophy or political science professorial colleagues has been able to tell me what is the nature of politics. In order for me to start my next book, I need to know what the definition of politics is.

D. Politics is the formulation and implementation of the rules of society.

H. That's it? Hmmm. Then, what would be the definition of ideology?

D. Ideology would be the denotation of how other people should live.

H. Well, if society is made up of individuals, how are these two definitions different?

D. Ideology sits inside politics. Ideology is an intellectual exercise by which the participants formulate a strategy for how other people should live. The actual implementation of how other people should live within a particular society is politics.

H. I think I understand. Let's say, for instance, a guy named Lenin is just sitting around and has formulated these ideas he got from a guy named Karl Marx and he believes that those rules that Karl Marx described should be implemented for his society. Therefore, the particular rules of Marxism are his ideology, and the implementation of the ideology into his society, known as Russia, would be politics.

D. Right.

H. The ideology of the United States would be described in the U.S. Constitution and the Bill of Rights which, for example, states in the Fifth Amendment, among other decrees, that no person shall be deprived of life, liberty, or property without due process of law; and secondly, the politics of the United States would be the debate and implementation of the Constitution, the rules, and the laws that are made by the government.

D. Excellent!

H. So, what other ideologies are there? What are the politics and ideologies of Islam?

D. Yeah, that's a good one to define: the ideology of Islam would be the rules and regulations set forth in the Quran and the Hadith (and the jurisprudence of Sharia Law); and the implementation of this in society would be the politics of Islam.

H. And what would be the politics and ideology of a fascist country?

D. Fascism is the ideology that the state should own, or control, the major means of production; and of course, the implementation of that is the politics of fascism; and this is the typical ideology of totalitarian governments.

H. And socialism?

D. Socialism is related to fascism but just on the other end of the spectrum. Socialism doesn't care about who owns the means of production; it just cares about who owns the results of the production. So, if the heads of society produce either goods or services through profitable corporations, then the socialist will tax that profit from the corporations and re-distribute it to society using any of its socialist progressive priorities it may have.

H. And communism would be that the workers of society own the means to production ... supposedly.

D. Right, and of course, the State will intervene, naturally, to hold the means to production in trust for the workers of society because the State is so trustworthy, to be a little bit sarcastic.

H. Noted and appreciated. So, the rules, regulations, and laws that a society generates in its political negotiations produce these priorities of socialism, fascism, communism, and so forth which represent some of the ideologies of the world.

D. That's right.

H. Oh yes, and one more thing: we have to define oligarchy also; and I'll give that a try as I've read from textbooks that an oligarchy is the control of society by a few individuals.

D. Right.

H. And so, an oligarchy is similar to fascism in that the means to production are owned by a few. So, instead of the state, an oligarchy is a few individuals that control the government making them immensely wealthy.

D. Yes, I think most textbooks would agree with our summation here of the various types of governments and their ideologies that result from a society's rules, regulations, and laws.

H. So really, the difference between all these types of ideologies (or should I say political ideologies) involves the type, amount, and the placement of the control of society's production of its goods and services.

D. Excellent! Very perceptive! Control dictates the type of ideology a society may have.

H. Well, if control dictates the type of society - or political society - then what dictates the essence of being a Leftist or a Rightist? What is a liberal, progressive Leftist, and what is a conservative person of the Right?

D. Again, the amount and placement of control dictate how the politics will differ.

H. What!? Is it that the only difference between the Left and the Right, such as between a Democrat and a Republican, here in the United States, would be the essence of the amount and placement of control that one party or the other chooses to place upon society?

D. Yes.

H. Well, I always thought from my readings and textbooks that the basic difference between a Democrat and a Republican is that the Democrat (or liberal) would believe that the federal government should help with the problems of society while the Republican (or conservative) would believe that societal problems should be first addressed at the local government level, then the state level, and lastly at the federal government level. Is this correct? Or is it wrong?

D. It is correct in that it is an example of the manifestation of control. As you just stated, in the case of the Democrats, their efforts to address the problems of society begin with the accumulation of control in a central depository. The Republican believes that societal problems should be addressed by the control administered in a diffuse fashion at the local level: and thus, the control should be spread out and not concentrated, and should be diminished in magnitude at any particular point.

H. Well, I have a problem understanding where this will to control comes from and why it is all-important in the evolution of society; and now that I think about it, is it the one and only factor that differentiates the Left and the Right, which around here would be known as the difference between the Republican from the Democrat? Or maybe it shows what is the essential difference between a Republican and a Democrat. But, what is the origin of the difference between the Left and the Right?

D. The origin of the difference between the Left and the Right comes from seven Dictums of political philosophy. The first two are the will and desire that all life seeks that which is good for it and continually seeks that which is good for it; and the second Dictum is what Saint Augustine called Libido Dominandi, that is, the will to dominate. From these two Dictums comes the will to control others, but these two principles by themselves do not give us the magnitude of control.

H. OK, I can see that the first principle is absolutely true, that all life intends to seek that which is good for it; and I suppose it continually seeks that which is good for it on an ongoing basis. I have no problem with that because I know that I want to seek that which is good for me, and I continually desire that more goodness comes into my life now and in the future. It's pretty self-evident.

D. Right.

H. And, I remember the Saint Augustine principle from reading

13

the *City of God.* I recall the principle of Libido Dominandi whereby Saint Augustine says that man likes to dominate others and that there's a will for one to naturally want to dominate the other. Also, I've read a fair amount of biological anthropology, and it basically says the same thing. In comparative behavior studies, we can see in various species that act in groups that there is an alpha male that tends to rise above the others in order to dominate the herd, or troop, to mate with the females so as to further his genetics into the next generation. Of course, Saint Augustine didn't have the luxury of comparative biological and anthropological studies to help him with this theory, but obviously, he was able to discern it and divine it on his own through his observation of the human species. It's clear that man (along with many other species) has the behavioral trait of the tendency to want to dominate others.

D. That's right.

H. Yes, I think we can rely on St. Augustine's principle as it has the confirmation of the various biological anthropological studies to confirm its verity.

D. And so, from these two first principles of political philosophy, it naturally occurs, even in primitive societies, that, at least, one person will try to dominate the group with enough knowledge or physical strength, or both, to become the leader of the group. He becomes a leader because, first, he wants that which is good for him; and further, he wants more goodness to come into his life. When you're the leader, you may extract from the group and from your environment more goodness than that which is available to the other societal members. Secondly, you do it because of the will to dominate.

H. Naturally, there'll be others wanting to do the same, and so, there'll be competition for first place in the group.

D. Exactly. We see this in nature in other species, and we see it in mankind. We observe it at the beginnings of tribal societies, continuing up to the complex nations of today. All throughout, these two Dictums are at work.

H. Yes, I can see that. In all societies throughout history, there has been one who always rises and becomes the leader. All the groups, all the sodalities have a leader. There have been some groups like communes that might not have had a leader, but these societies always are temporary and fail eventually.

D. Yes, that's correct. They all failed.

H. One interesting tome that I read was Sir Thomas More's book, *Utopia*. I remember reading it and thinking this is impossible. If an utopian society without private property could really exist, the people there in Hythloday's society would not be the human beings that I know. I remember reading the work and remarking that there is one thing lacking in his Utopia: and that is that there is no motivation for the individual to do what they do which is to help each other incessantly, with no limit, without reserve, and without reward. And, I now see your point that all of life strives for that which is good for it; and if there's no reward in one's sacrifice but only the utopian reward of the satisfaction of knowing that you did something good for somebody else, then perhaps, it works temporarily, but it will not work as a modus operandi for societal denizens on a continual basis. Without motivation, without life being able to receive that goodness that it seeks for its sacrifices, any society would not do well. Also, I remember when we spoke about this in my fourth book, *The Philosophical*

Equations of Economics: all of life makes sacrifices in order to receive a reward.

D. Yes, the relationship between the sacrifice and the reward establishes the motivation. A small sacrifice with the opportunity of a great reward increases the motivation. A large sacrifice comparative to a small reward decreases the motivation, and so it is in the book, *Utopia*: the reward to the individual that is to be received from the various sacrifices in helping and assisting others is diminished down only to the pure satisfaction of knowing that you did well for somebody else. And when the reward is small - and continually small - compared to the sacrifice of the individuals of society, the will to assist others will eventually diminish. The denizens will always weigh the sacrifice relative to the size of the reward.

H. Yes, understood. I can see that these two principles existed throughout all times, throughout all societies, without exception, necessarily.

D. And, from these first two principles of political philosophy, the first two political parties evolved.

H. So, from the first two Dictums, we have two political parties?

D. Yes, we have the two political parties consisting of the Haves and the Have-Nots. We could also call them the two political parties of the Leader and the Followers, but I prefer the Haves and the Have-Nots. The Haves are the leaders of society, and the Have-Nots are those that either work for the leaders or just have less than the leaders because the leaders demand some sort of tribute. In rudimentary societies, it would be the elder or the leader of the tribe; and then, in the more advanced societies (which would be a super-tribe, whereby the leader no longer knows each

16

individual member of the tribe as the zoological anthropologist Desmond Morris denoted), the Haves would be the king and the queen and below them would be the Have-Nots which would be the serfs, the proletariats, the slaves, the workers.

H. Yes, I can see that.

D. As society advances and the number of individuals within the societies increases, the king and queen require assistance in being able to administer to the proletariat and the slaves efficiently. They would need help. Hence, the class of the nobles appears.

H. OK, I can see that. The kings and queens of the super-tribes will need help in administering their policies that they want to implement which is, of course, to control the lower class of people that farm the land and make the various goods and services of society and to expand their society as opportunities arise, as per Dictums 1 and 2. This situation has existed throughout history.

D. As society even further grows, the nobles require further assistance, and they will make a group of facilitators known as government bureaucrats to help administer their policies which are issued from the policies of the king and queen, by edicts put out by the nobles, and the rules and regulations of the facilitators of the nobles.

H. And, as societies grow and become nations, then these groups become larger and more powerful. But what happens to the Have-Nots during this time? They seem to become better off over time.

D. Yes, they do, and it is due to the first two Dictums of political philosophy that we just discussed, namely, that all life wants that which is good for it and continually wants that which is good for it on an ongoing basis, and secondly, all life wants to dominate; and because all life wants to dominate, humans are well adapted to competition with each willing to compete with the other.

H. But, how do they get out of the proletariat, serfdom, or slavery class? How do they rise up out of that?

D. They will do whatever it takes to seek goodness for their lives. There are many ways for the serfs to come out of their low-class status and rise up to a middle class in trying to seek goodness for themselves. One way is to revolt, and there are many famous revolts throughout history. Look at Spartacus, the Maccabean Revolt, the English Revolutions, the American Revolution, the French Revolutions, and others. Another way is to invent something. We invent things in order to bring goodness into our lives and the goodness consists of an efficiency in being able to receive a reward (or a greater reward) for our sacrifices into our lives which is the basis of all of economics. For society to become more advanced, it requires efficiencies made by the societal members that make society more efficacious producing more with less.

H. Yes, that's true. All economies advance, as we studied before in *The Philosophical Equations of Economics*, through the improving of the ingredients of the sacrifice to become better off. Those ingredients to the sacrifice are the risk, the information and knowledge, the time, the effort, and material that we experience and expend in making our sacrifice in order to achieve a reward.

D. Yes.

H. Hence, there are ways that economic activity can be improved: first is increasing the number of sacrifices, that is, there would be an increasing number of sacrifices altogether; increasing the variables of the sacrifice such as the time people can spend on their sacrifices; increase the effort of the sacrifice; reduce the risk involved; increase material (if it is a product); or increase knowledge. The increase in knowledge is a little bit different in that it provides not just a sheer increase in the quantity of economic activity, but it can generate efficiencies to be introduced into the economy. And, this is 99% of the way economies grow.

D. That's right.

H. The application of knowledge to the sacrifice that we make in order to receive a reward is the way that an economy grows almost entirely. Societies grow almost entirely through technological and cerebral advancements which are forms of knowledge that produce all the increased economic activity through the efficiencies that it brings to the basic economic transaction.

D. Most certainly. Hence, we have two political classes from which all political parties derive. We have the Haves and the Have-Nots, and both the Haves and the Have-Nots are subject to Dictums 1 and 2. Dictum 1, again, is that all life seeks that which is good for it and continually wants that which is good for it. It is not enough to achieve goodness and not want more. All life seeks more. Therefore, mankind wants to jump out of the slavery and proletariat class (or classes if you prefer). Both the Haves and the Have-Nots seek more goodness.

H. Yes, I understand.

D. In rising to the position of tribal leader, they are subject to Dictum 2 which is that of dominance. They come out of their class to prevail and compete with others thereby becoming the predominating faction that we are nominating here as the Haves. And, the Have-Nots, meanwhile, strive to jump out to go to the middle class, or the bourgeois class, and in doing so, they are also subject to Dictum 2 because inevitably those that jump out will dominate other workers, their families, groups, companies, corporations, organizations, and so forth.

H. Yes, I understand Libido Dominandi. And even the Have-Nots are subject to it because when they create an efficiency in their lives from their invention of the new product or service that leads to a better life, they often come together to create companies to be able to produce the new goods and services, and in doing so, somebody has to be a boss, and naturally, the person who created the company is subject to Dictum 2 and will want to control what he has created and oversee the production of goods and services that he has sufficiently brought to bear upon his local economy. Therefore, I can see the origin of societies whereby there is a society with a king and queen and with a low class consisting of the slaves, proletariats, serfs, and so forth, doing the menial labor. Then, there's a new class that pops out due to knowledge proliferating and producing efficiencies from which a new middle class (a.k.a. the bourgeoisie) is born.

D. Right!

H. The number of classes we have at this point is five. We have those who garner and aggregate to themselves as much of the wealth of society for their own goodness, which are society's king and queen. Second in command is the noble class. The nobles are the first line of facilitators to impress upon the lower classes the policies and regulations by which society must operate. Next in line as the society grows are the facilitators who also could be known as the bureaucratic class in larger societies. This is made up of the regulators that assist the nobles in administering the laws, regulations, and rules emanating from the upper classes. So, as I see it, we have five classes so far: the king and queen, the nobles, and the facilitators which are the classes of the Haves, and the middle and the lower classes, such as the serfs, proles, slaves, of the Haves-Nots.

D. That's exactly right.

H. OK, where do we go from here?

D. This system of classes is a natural progression of societal evolution.

H. How so?

D. Because of the first two principles of political philosophy, societies, ever since the dawn of man, naturally have devolved into this situation. All we have to do is look back through all of history to see the result of this class situation.

H. OK, but there have been a couple of partial exceptions, I think, such as the direct Athenian democracy of ancient Greece which did not have a king and queen class and where the concept of citizenship may have started; and I think we can add in the Roman Empire to some extent, with its creation of the Senate and its developing concept of citizenship. Rome instituted the idea of citizen rights, created by Roman law, by which its law conferred upon its denizens rights to become a citizen that distinguished the citizen from the slave. So, there were some advancements in history. After all, Roman law is the basis for English common law.

D. That's right! And the reason why the rights of the citizen and the idea of citizenry developed in rudimentary societies is that it facilitated the development of knowledge which created efficiencies in the economy. As these efficiencies grow and society becomes wealthier, and as those who develop those efficiencies become more valuable to society and have to be recognized even by the king and queen which they will want to do because of Dictum 1, the Haves will recognize that the newly-developing societal goodness will additionally accrue to themselves also.

H. Is that necessarily so?

D. It is, for two reasons: knowledge cannot be created, replicated, and learned easily; and secondly, it cannot be entirely deposited in one central depository of knowledge. It is more efficient to keep knowledge, as it grows and becomes abundant throughout society, dispersed amongst the citizenry as there is no one person that can maintain, control, and administer all of the knowledge.

H. Of course, there are famous philosopher-economists that would agree with that statement.

D. As these efficiencies grow within society, the king and queen will recognize the importance of those individuals that hold the knowledge of efficiencies that enable the production of all the goods and services that society creates; and it would be understood and recognized that these people become more and more important to society.

H. I see.

D. Consequently, due mainly to knowledge there grows an interdependency between the upper classes that want all goodness and the lower classes that provide the goodness of the labor, the goods, services, efficiencies, and improvements of society. As such, the upper societal classes must tolerate the new middle and lower classes.

H. Tolerate?

D. That's right. They tolerate these lower classes for all the goodness they produce; but they will not relinquish their control that they operate on the lower classes due to Dictums 1 and 2. The maintenance of their control is required to ensure that they will be able to confiscate and self-appropriate a consistent portion of the goodness of the lower classes' production. Dictum 1 is a powerful motivator.

H. Professor, that is interesting, and this is certainly consistent with history.

D. The upper classes never produced much while it was always the lower classes – the serfs, the slaves, the laborers that did all the work and production of society. Even the geniuses of society were originally of the lower classes. The king, queen, and the nobility throughout history created very little except maybe war, oppression, laws, immorality, regulations, and taxes while, of course, plundering the lower classes of their production.

H. Professor, you sound like some sort of a Marxist. But, I know better from our previous conversations which I nominated as *The Philosophical Equations of Economics*. I know, that within these lower classes of the serfs and slaves of history, there arose the middle classes from the economic efficiencies that it produced and eventually the right of possession (a.k.a. property rights) which originally only dwelt within, first, the royal class, then within the noble class eventually, and next was extended to the middle class because of the inter-cooperative reliance on each other that developed between the upper classes and the middle class because of the new efficient valuable goods and services that the lower classes began to produce by the entrepreneurs and because of the

23

knowledge of the lower classes which is generated by the power of the first political principle, Dictum 1.

D. Well said.

Chapter 2: The Dictums of the Haves

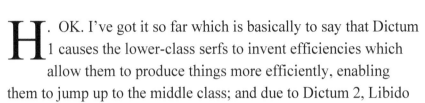

H. OK. I've got it so far which is basically to say that Dictum 1 causes the lower-class serfs to invent efficiencies which allow them to produce things more efficiently, enabling them to jump up to the middle class; and due to Dictum 2, Libido Dominandi, the upper class will yet want to continue to maintain control of both the serf and middle classes.

D. Right.

H. But you mentioned there are seven Dictums of political philosophy altogether.

D. Yes, in addition to Dictums 1 and 2, which propels the upper class to dominate, there is an additional propensity to control the lower classes by another Dictum which is that the upper class believes that the lower classes have a nature that is not good.

H. What?

D. The upper classes throughout history have always looked down on the lower classes as being inferior, not being of royal blood, not being of noble birth, and not having a good nature. These lower classes are all within the deplorable class as those of the lower classes are comprised of low character and a bad inherent nature.

H. Yes, you are right. Throughout history, the upper classes have always looked down on the working classes, the deplorables. I am reminded of the famous statement of Rousseau's great princess, "Let them eat cake (brioches)."

D. So, Dictum 3 is that the Haves believe that the Have-Nots are inherently bad people. The Haves believe that the Have-Nots are by their nature not good, and so they cannot be trusted to do good things. In fact, they (the Have-Nots) can often be considered evil.

H. Wow! How can this be? Well, maybe throughout history it has been that way; but how can ever in America, the home of the brave, the land of the free, can one group of people consider the others to be, by their essence, bad?

D. The thoughts of history are powerful, and this will make some sense if we merge these Dictums 1 and 2. A leader rises to the top because of these Dictums and wants to stay at the top in a leadership position because he/she, through establishing control of others, has the lion's share of the goodness of the societal production, and then, for some reason begins to perceive, due to his/her presence in a leadership position, that they, the king and queen, are more important than others because they have the responsibility to command society; and they come to believe that they are better than others in society. They, the king and queen, are most important; and naturally, their facilitators, the nobles, are almost as good. Hence, this hierarchy of goodness descends downward in a decreasing manner with the king and queen (their Highnesses) having the most goodness, the nobles being second, the public functionary next in goodness of self-perceived, societal, royal goodness until we arrive at the non-governmental classes. These governmental caste classes due to Dictums 1 and 2 will seek to control those below them in the pecking order and do so for their own benefit. They (the controlling classes) will look down on the lower classes and perceive the lower classes as being of lesser worth all the while perceiving themselves as great.

H. But why? Why should it be this way? Why should the royalty look down on the lower and middle classes perceiving them as having little worth? Why should these lower-class people be seen as the deplorables or irredeemables and not worthy to be of the upper classes? Why should this type of thought come to be? Why would you need royal blood in order to become one of the royal classes? And why does this system of thought even pervade the American society, albeit to a lesser extent than other societies of yore, that those with societal power are more important than others who are not of ruling status? But nonetheless, we can even see it in the speeches of the political governing class calling the common man pejoratives such as "the deplorables." Why?

D. Because of Dictum 5.

H. And, what of this Dictum 5, pray tell? And by the way, what happened to Dictum 4?

D. We will skip Dictum 4 for the nonce. Dictum 5 is the famous truism of Lord Acton: Power tends to corrupt, and absolute power corrupts absolutely.

H. How does this work itself into our philosophical Dictums of politics making it now our fifth principle?

D. It is because of the existence of the nature of cooperation.

H. Really? I know that evolution has developed an ability to cooperate among much of life, all the way from ants up to mankind. Much of life has developed the facility of cooperation, and we know from one of my previous works developed from my notes of the conversations with you, Professor, that cooperation is the basis for man's development of his sense of ethics. We know from my second work, *The Nature of Ethics: Defining Ethics Good & Evil*, that ethics is the appropriate dispensation of respect.

D. Right.

H. If we treat somebody with the appropriate amount of respect, then our behavior toward that person is ethical. As an example, if we treat our parents with respect, then our actions are ethical. If we treat our boss at work with respect, then we are being ethical toward him.

D. Correct.

H. Respect is the evolutionary means by which we are able to cooperate; and we cooperate in order to produce goods and services; and we produce to receive goodness and that which is good is that which brings this up away from misery, which is the nature of all that is good.

D. Yes.

H. So, how is the nature of cooperation related to our new Dictum?

D. It is that we cooperate because we realize that we can produce more goods and services, more efficiently, by cooperating with others than if we were to do it alone. Cooperation allows us to be more efficient in our production of goodness; it allows us to be special beings not only for the purpose of production of goods and services but also for the production of social happiness as well as being able to live in society in general.

H. OK.

D. When one cooperates with another, we do so by creating an agreement, covenant, contract, or some sort of mutual understanding of how to work together to produce a good or service, or to produce social happiness such as to be friends, which we, or others, want in order to make our lives better. Within this action of creating an understanding comes the ordering of the division of the components of this mutual transaction of making a sacrifice to obtain a reward. As we know from our previous conversation noted in your *The Philosophical Equations of Economics,* the components are time, information/knowledge, risk, and effort for a service; and if it is a physical item, then we add material as one of the components to our sacrifice to obtain a reward.

H. Yes.

D. And when we cooperate, we are adding, to some degree, to one or more of the components of a sacrifice to receive a reward which is the objective of our sacrifice. Thus, the more we cooperate, the more we are in unison in the sacrifice to produce a reward which is the opposite of corruption.

H. Why is it the opposite?

D. It is the opposite because corruption is the taking of the sacrifice of others for the benefit of oneself.

H. Then, corruption is a kind of theft.

D. And so power breeds corruption because with power comes the ability to coerce, and so the person or entity that acquires the ability to coerce accrues the propensity to forsake cooperation. That entity can just coerce others to acquire the goods and services of others, doing so in order to bypass the effort of providing any degree of the ingredients in the cooperative sacrifice that others would do together to produce a reward that will bring goodness to one's life.

H. Interesting.

D. But, there's another reason why absolute power corrupts absolutely, and it has to do with the nature of freedom and our priorities.

H. OK, let's review what is the nature of freedom.

D. Freedom is the construction of priorities supplemented with the effectuation of those priorities; and as you discussed in your third book, decision-making comes from the construction of a priority in the consciousness. As an example, when sometime during each day we get hungry, the pangs of hunger occur, and as such, we seek remedies against that occurrence because as the day drags on, the hunger does not go away, but increases, and the pangs of hunger increase to the point where we are consumed with this priority to quell these feelings.

H. Yes. This is the construction of a priority to make a decision.

D. Hence, we've constructed a priority, that is a piece of knowledge, which is that we know we want to quell our hunger. And so, we do. We go about the execution of that priority by going to the kitchen and looking for food, or perhaps going down to the grocery store and buying food, or perhaps going to a restaurant and ordering something to alleviate the hunger. Each of these actions is an effectuation of the priority which is to eat so that we can feel good again with a full stomach.

H. Thus, freedom is comprised of two actions: the construction of the priority which is a piece of knowledge, and then the effectuation of the priority which is the second action.

D. As mentioned, after we've constructed the priority which is a piece of knowledge, we have to decide whether we want to effectuate the priority. In order to do this, we have to construct our equation of the sacrifice versus the reward. Each sacrifice is made up of risk, information/knowledge, time, effort, and material if it's going to be a product that is being produced by the sacrifice. As these elements make up the sacrifice, they will also make up the reward side of the equation as a reward also consists of risk, knowledge, time, and effort which is the result of the sacrifice that we do to produce a good or service making the reward available for acquisition.

H. Yes, I remember.

D. And now, in order to complete the decision, a comparison of the sacrifice and the amount of the reward to be received has to be compared. The individual decision-maker will compare the elements that make up the sacrifice with the elements that make up the reward; and if that sacrifice is little and the reward is great, the motivation to go ahead and make the sacrifice to receive the reward will be great. Therefore, to make any decision, the comparison of the sacrifice relative to the reward must be established to know the motivation present for the individual to decide whether to go ahead with his decision and effectuate his priority, and this all happens throughout our lives as we seek that which is good for us.

H. OK, that sounds rational. It's natural that we need to be motivated in order to do what we do. Actually, it seems like all of life must make this motivational equation in order to make a decision, calculating the risk, effort, and time to make the sacrifice to achieve the reward. It is the comparison of the sacrifice relative to the reward that provides the motivation.

D. Well, it is here that absolute power corrupts absolutely; and it is because the motivational factors become skewed.

H. How's that?

D. For the Royal-Haves, the risk factors become skewed because cooperation is no longer needed. As such, the risk becomes negligible relative to the reward for a totalitarian leader. The more control that the leader has, the more he may reduce his risk as he has superior control due to the fact that there's no longer a contract in place between himself and the rest of society. Ergo, the risk of the sacrifice becomes artificially low as the king and queen can unilaterally depreciate the amount of risk inherent in their sacrifice in order to obtain the reward that they seek. They don't have to negotiate any agreements when you have full control over society. If they have full control, or totalitarian control, they could just declare that everybody will work as slaves, and they don't have to work at all reducing their risk to obtain whatever it was that they seek.

H. So, it could be something very serious like in the case of war whereby the leadership of a country wants to go to war; and if they're in total control, then the rest of society's influence is very small; and even though the lower classes may choose not to go into the war, it is not their decision because the totalitarian decision-makers do not have to seek cooperation. All the deplorables, serfs, and the people of the lower class will do the fighting and endure the danger and risk, and do their bidding in the war theater.

D. That is correct. The great progenitors of war all had this situation before they committed their denizens of society to their horrible objectives. Let's take an example, such as Hitler. Once he gained total control of his country through the declaration of a national emergency, he would marshal the entire nation at his behest because it was no longer democratic, and no longer did the people have a say in what avenue the nation could direct itself. Therefore, under his totalitarian rule, Hitler could make his objectives a reality; that is, he could effectuate his priorities by ordering the military and the nation to mobilize under his directives. He could do this without risk to himself because he was in total control. No longer is there any agreement or cooperative necessity between himself, the Führer, and the rest of the nation. He did not have to fight. And so, his mind becomes corrupted totally and absolutely as cooperative behavior is not required, nor welcome.

H. As such, the same would be true for Japan's decision to enter the war (against the United States). They were totalitarian in nature with the military and the emperor controlling the societal denizens. The people had no say. There was no contract in place. No cooperative rights to protect the people. And so, control corrupted the mind of the leaders, and they could enter a war with all its devastating effects on all nations involved. Yes, Lord Acton's principle reigns supreme: these totalitarian leaders with their absolute power become mentally corrupted by doing that which is good for themselves by effectuating their own priorities without regard to others and without regard to having to cooperate in any agreements involved with the nation over which they rule.

D. Japan was governed by the royal, imperial Haves which included, essentially, the emperor and the military, and naturally, they sought goodness for themselves and for the nation of Japan, Dictum 1. Secondly, they not only had the will to dominate their country but also the entire Asian region of the world (Dictum 2) to which the Japanese military would bring their Japanese culture and domination which is a result of their corrupted point of view resulting from Dictum 5. Thirdly, the Japanese royalty believed that the end justifies the means because they had no respect for those outside of their culture who were the Have-Nots which was due to Dictum 3 that the Have-Nots were inherently not good because they were the barbarians from without. Ergo, those outside their culture needed to be controlled as per Dictum 3. To this, we add to the Japanese military the motivation to venture out perpetrating their military adventurism and atrocities throughout Asia and to eventually Pearl Harbor.

H. Understood. Subsequently, of course, the U.S. responded naturally. By the way, I noticed a pretty important word in our conversation which is, "control." Would you be able to define that?

D. Control is a unilateral contract plus force. It is the supplanting by force the priorities of oneself for the priorities of the other.

H. Let's go over the nature of control itself and its relationship to our list of the philosophical Dictums of politics.

D. The purpose of the seven Dictums of the political philosophy of the Haves is to foster and maintain control over the Have-Nots.

H. Let's review this a little bit. I understand the first three. The first principle is that life does that which is good for it. And naturally, the Haves want to do what is best for the Haves, no exception. So, if they can rise to the top, become royalty, and take a portion - or a goodly portion - of the societal products and services, they will do so. The second principle is the domination factor, and in this case, people necessarily want to rise up above others, and we all strive to do so or at least have a natural inclination to do so. These two in combination indicate that somebody within society will intend to rise up, become a Have, keep what he has, and try to maintain this situation as long as possible to bring as much good to himself as possible; and then thirdly, we've discussed that the Haves possess an innate view of the Have-Nots that dictates or induces them to view others as not having a good heart (Dictum 3). The Haves believe that they (the Have-Nots) are not by nature essentially good and that they are inherently bad people. This will allow the Haves to include facilitators to keep the Have-Nots where they are and allow the Haves to proliferate and enjoy the goodness of society.

D. That's right, and this is why we sometimes hear the statement by the extreme progressive Leftists that they hate America which is to say that this country is filled with the deplorable's, and they need to be subdued, but they are not!

H. But I know there's more to the story because I know that there are other Dictums as you had mentioned that there are seven in total.

D. The next one up is the Dictum of Noblesse Oblige which we will call Dictum 4. This Dictum says that the Haves know that they have an obligation to the Have-Nots and that they must provide a minimum lifestyle to the Have-Nots. The Haves know that they have an obligation to provide a base or minimum standard of living which they need to provide to the Have-Nots, and from this evolved the ideologies of control, such as Marxism, Communism, Fascism, and Socialism; that is, the base, lower classes need to be provided with a minimum standard of living.

H. But, this was not always the case throughout history. This concept didn't come into being until the first half of the 19th century. Before that, the serfs and the other Have-Nots were very much looked down upon and had almost nothing. To understand this, all we have to do is look back to the Middle Ages and see how deprived the lower class of the caste societies lived. They were very poor: the serfs, the slaves, the proletariats, the downtrodden. Anybody in those lower classes was of a minimal lifestyle. It wasn't until the rise of the middle class that some people started to become a little better off.

D. The concept of Noblesse Oblige arose because of the revolutions, particularly the French Revolutions, which indicated to the nobles that they could only go so far in their oppression of the lower classes. So, they learned. And, what came about are the societies of the Left, such as communism, Marxism, fascism, and socialism.

H. As I know from my reading some history, Marxism and communism required theoretically, total control of society by the lower classes, and this ideology came about because the aristocracy treated the working class with disdain and neglect throughout history allowing the idea of providing the lower classes an assurance that there is an obligation of the Haves to provide a minimal lifestyle for the workers. But from what I've read, it didn't work out too well, to say the least as the biggest slaughters of mankind in the 20th century were imposed upon societies by the various Haves, which came to control their societies with their revolutions and replaced the previous Royalty with their new brand of being the new Haves of society. They were the communists, or should I say the Marxists. There was Stalin who some say caused the death of as many as fifty million people, and then there was Mao Zedong who did the same in China, and then there were others such as Pol Pot. All were, in essence, the ultimate Leftist-Haves.

D. That's right, and so the ultimate arbiter of all that is the Left and all of the progressive, liberal, fascist, socialist movements of the Haves is guided by one factor which is the amount of control that the Haves would seek over the lower classes. The more control that the Haves seek and obtain, the more that they are of the Left; and as such, there are various degrees of the Left.

H. I think I can agree with that.

D. An example of somebody who we might think of as, what I will call, "leftist-lite" or "center-left" would be presidents like Bill Clinton, John F. Kennedy, or Harry Truman. These are Democrats who tried to enlarge the control of society but only incrementally and are almost indistinguishable from the "center-right Republican." Kennedy and Clinton actually decreased taxes and Clinton initiated, along with a Republican Congress, a work-for-welfare program.

H. Probably the next one down the line would be Lyndon Baines Johnson with his Great Society and then Franklin Roosevelt in the 1930s with his various government-sponsored socialist programs such as the National Recovery Act and others that attempted to take even more control of society. But some of his centralized control programs were struck down by the Supreme Court; then World War II followed, so he was never able to fully initiate his socialist controlling views on American society. Maybe we could say that WWII actually forced FDR to reverse his policies in order to supply the machinery of war as the president had to cooperate with the major manufacturers that held the means to generate and produce the war supplies that the president and the nation needed to prosecute the war.

D. Then, we can move further to the Left with Mussolini and

Hitler who were fascists as they were totalitarian and wanted to govern even the means of production within their society. They wanted to manage everything to be able to control all of society.

H. The next step down the line of Leftism would be, of course, communism or Marxism which did not only control all the means to production but governed the very lives of the Have-Nots also whose stated purpose was to superintend the means to production to provide the Have-Nots with their lifestyles to protect them from the capitalist pigs. And I might say sarcastically that they were sure good at that. The communists and the totalitarians were very effective at controlling all aspects of society.

D. Yes, that's correct, and so the amount of governance that the royal, the noble, and facilitator classes have at their disposal to administer to the lower classes of society is the determining factor of the degree to which the Leftist-Haves are controlling. The concept of Noblesse Oblige only contributed to the fervency of how much the Haves should effectuate control of the Have-Nots by feeding their altruistic sense of providing for the lower class a minimum standard of living, or in other words, the initiation of the social net.

H. Interesting.

D. The idea of initiating and providing a socialistic welfare-oriented society allows the Leftist-Haves to be moralistic and righteous in their will to bring goodness to society with this social net. Subsequently, the Democrat believes that they have the higher moral ground because they care for their fellow humans and desire to provide a social net. It is the one factor that goes through all the thoughts of the Democrats, Leftists, Socialists, Communists, and Progressives and allows them to proceed to the moral high ground. This Dictum of the social net is the primary principle that tends to make their morality thinking worse and all-consuming, leading to the quest for more control of society.

H. I have noticed this, and it is my opinion that governments throughout the world - including the one of the United States - tend to move left and not right. Overall, they tend to become more liberal, Left-leaning; and it probably is from this concept of providing a social net for the lower classes for the poor people of the world that leads them to become Democrats, Leftists, Marxists, Communists, or any other degree of Leftism. It appears to be their raison d'être, and it all originates from this Noblesse Oblige concept that you just mentioned as the fourth principle of political philosophy.

D. There is a multi-pronged reason why they move to the Left after society's initial lurch to the Right which was caused by a revolution whereby the Haves give up rights to the Have-Nots through a revolution. It is not only because of Dictum 4 but because it is in combination with Dictum 3 that the other person has a bad heart. As we mentioned, the Haves - or in modern times, the Leftists - believe that the nature of the lower classes is that it is comprised of those with whom they do not have to cooperate, that have an evil heart and are inherently bad people. Therefore, the Democrats negotiate with Republicans while viewing the Republicans as having an inherently bad heart or nature. Hence, they don't want to give up anything that they've established because to do so is to acquiesce to those who are bad (or even evil) which is in itself a very bad thing. To reiterate, they have the high moral ground in their eyes.

H. Curiously, when society gets the inkling to move Right to the policies of the Have-Nots, the Leftist-Haves become intractable;

and if it actually does start to move Right, heading back whence it originally came at the founding of the country, the Left begins to boil generating vitriolic rhetoric, outright lies, tantrums, and eventually violence if they don't get their way. If I were to mention this to anybody on the Left, they would retort that both sides do it; but it is not true should we refer to a general historical comparison according to my readings.

D. And, the Republicans, Conservatives, or those who originate from the Have-Nots, believe that in general, the other people are basically good people and that their nature is inherently good which is their Dictum 3. So, when they are negotiating with the Democrats, they try to find something that is good about the policy that is being discussed. So, one side tries to look to find something that's good about it and they're willing to compromise over it, while the other side is not so willing to compromise, because they think that the other side is inherently bad. So, the Left, in general, is less willing to compromise, and each time a compromise is made, it tends to go to the Left because of their adherence to Dictum 3.

H. And, what about the last two Dictums? Where will that leave us?

D. Dictum 6 explains the ethics of the Left and the Right. The control-oriented Leftist-Haves approach the problems of politically dealing with the other person in that they believe that the end justifies the means, which is, as Lord Acton pointed out, as he said: "Great men are almost always bad men, even when they exercise influence and not authority: still more when you superadd the tendency or the certainty of corruption by authority. There is no worse heresy than the office sanctifying the holder of it. That is the point at which the negation of Catholicism and the negation of

Liberalism meet and keep high festival, and the end learns to justify the means."

H. Profound.

D. Meanwhile, the Right believes that one should be ethical to the common man in the classical sense of ethics which we discussed in your book, *The Nature of Ethics: Defining Ethics, Good and Evil.*

H. OK, so the Right believes that ethics is the appropriate dispensation of respect. And we respect others in order to be able to cooperate with them, and we cooperate with others to be able to produce more efficiently goods and services; and we want to do so because it makes our life better which fulfills Dictum 1 allowing us to bring more goodness into our lives, which brings us up away from misery, which is the essence of goodness.

D. All six of them describe the philosophical actions and beliefs of the Left. And finally, there is Dictum 7 which is that the Haves always seek more control of others, yet more freedom for themselves.

H. And, what about the Right? What dictums dictate their political actions and thoughts?

D. Dictums 1 and 2 are the same because these pervade the entire human race, indeed all of life. Dictum 3 declares that the Left believes that the hearts of others who are not of the Left (and in some cases even if they are of the Left) are bad; and the Right believes that the hearts of others are good, or essentially good, which presents the first dichotomy between the two types of political thought.

41

H. I see. Dictum 3 presents the polar opposite of the two sides of political thought. I guess that essentially the Leftist-Haves look at the human race as being inherently bad, and the conservative Have-Not side looks at the human race as inherently having a good nature. This would allow the Left to always find fault with anything. After all, the other person is inherently bad by his nature; therefore, whatever the idea, the conservative must be bad.

D. Even if something is 99% good, they will fault it because it is not perfect; but nothing is perfect so they will always criticize unless it is their idea that will further the control of society or something that is related to their Noblesse Oblige contract.

H. So, they have their view that the other guy outside of their team is by his nature bad or even evil. (Let's recall from my previous book on ethics which stated that evil is an unethical action combined with an unethical objective.) And their view has credence from a Biblical point of view which teaches us that man is by nature a sinner, deals in trespasses and sins, is alienated from God, and is altogether corrupt. As St. Paul said, "As it is written, There is none righteous, no, not one ... there is none that doeth good, no, not one." (KJV)

D. Both sides have a legitimate point of view. The Left side concurs with the biblical outlook that everybody has sinned, and we all come short of the glory of God. Man is sinful. The Right side looks at the good side as Jesus did. Jesus declared that he would make his disciples fishers of men and he did. He wouldn't have done it unless he thought that his disciples would accept him and his teachings, would go out, and do good by spreading the word of the good news. Jesus would not have come into his ministry and done his work without thinking that man could be saved by belief in his teachings, and as such, has a good side and could be trusted to spread the good news.

H. Let's see if I can succinctly analyze the situation. First, we must realize that we sacrifice our time and effort, and use our knowledge and information, in an atmosphere of risk in order to get the rewards that allow us to live and obtain goodness. (We detailed this in my work, *The Philosophical Equations of Economics*.) Next, we must add in the teachings of Paul (as per my understanding of them). God has love for mankind even though we are sinners and by his grace God can give to mankind salvation freely and mercifully through the ministry of Christ Jesus. In response to his ministry, we proffer our faith in Christ, and in return as a reward, we get salvation. And this opportunity is presented because Christ makes an horrific sacrifice of his life under torture in order for us to receive the reward of salvation as all of life is a series of transactions, whereby we make sacrifices in order to receive rewards.

D. So, God freely gives, through love, the teachings and sacrifice of Christ, which was painful, making it a true sacrifice without expecting anything in return because it is through his grace that we may receive it; and if we accept the sacrifice of Christ, then we may receive salvation. And for those of mankind that can accept and believe in this scenario, then there is goodness within them, and it is that goodness that the conservative believes is inherent in the nature of mankind. Further, St. Paul in Romans 6 teaches us that even though we are born in sin, that condition does not allow us to knowingly do bad things. Paul declares, "And having been set free from sin, you become slaves of righteousness."

H. And so, let me now move to the Have-Not version of the fourth Dictum of Noblesse Oblige. What would be the conservative side of this principle?

43

D. The conservative believes that instead of the Nobles through Noblesse Oblige having a contract with the Have-Nots to provide a base standard of living (of which the Haves are proud), there is a duty of the Have-Nots to sustain freedom and an adherence to effectuate freedom in society, promote the will to jump out of the Have-Not lower class, ascend to the middle, or Bourgeois, class to produce goodness for oneself and generate voluntary charity to the needy whenever possible.

H. This would be why the Left feels that they have the higher moral ground because it is a governmental obligation that they provide a minimal standard of living, whereas the conservative feels that it should be just a duty of voluntary charity generally; and thus, the needy might not be provided a social net at all because if it's voluntary, then the help might not get to the needy as somebody may just decide not to voluntarily be charitable in giving to the less fortunate.

D. Yes. And of course, the Left cannot brook that situation because they know that the heart and minds of the bourgeois middle and lower classes are fraught with those that are inherently bad as per Dictum 3; and thus cannot be entrusted with providing the basic needs for the lower class.

H. We covered the fifth Dictum, the Lord Acton Principle; and introduced Dictum 6 which is the nature of ethics which is the appropriate dispensation of respect.

D. However, in the case of the Leftists, it is the lack of ethics in that they believe that the end justifies the means, as Lord Acton pointed out.

H. And the end justifies the means is an immoral philosophy.

D. That's right; it is actually the absence of ethics. As you just mentioned, ethics is the appropriate dispensation of respect; and we respect others to be able to cooperate with them. Respect is the evolutionary aspect that allows us to cooperate with others. It does so by lowering the signs of aggression between those who want to cooperate. When you cooperate, you necessarily have to respect the other person for his knowledge, information, effort, awareness of risk, and time that he will put into the cooperative effort. We cooperate because we understand that we can do more together when producing a complicated product or service than if we were to do it by ourselves alone. We cooperate to produce goods and services because we realize that the other person is important, and so the consideration that we give to the other person is commensurate with our respect. Even in the case of money transactions, it is often said: in consideration for such and such products and services, we give a specific amount of dollars.

H. Yes, I remember this from my second book.

D. And, we produce goods and services in order to bring us up away from misery, which is the nature of good. That is, of course, for a commercial situation. But, the same is true for a social situation such as you respecting your parents. We do so because cooperation with them helps with your upbringing as your parents cooperated with you. After all, you are to succeed them and carry on their genetic information to the next generation.

H. OK, I understand that. But what about the end justifies the means? How does that fit into the nature of the Leftist ideology? Don't they want to cooperate also, and as such, dispense the appropriate degree of respect with whom they want to cooperate? They cooperate with others, and as such, would want to dispense the appropriate amount of respect for those with whom they want to cooperate.

D. Yes, of course. For those with whom they want to cooperate to produce a good or service, they dispense the appropriate amount of respect just as everybody does; and as such, they are ethical. But there's a problem, and that problem is in the political arena. Their Have ideology clashes with those of the Have-Not-Right as they wish no longer to be cooperative.

H. Why? I don't understand.

D. The Haves will turn away from ethical actions and the appropriate dispensation of respect in the political arena because of two principles that we discussed. First is the Lord Acton principle (Dictum 5) that absolute power breeds corruption absolutely. The Haves believe also that others inherently have a bad nature as per their Dictum 3. But when these two principles are combined, they produce a conclusive thought that it is not necessary to dispense the appropriate amount of respect. If respect is not required, then all that remains is the end justifies the means.

H. How so?

D. First, the Haves believe that those who are not of the Haves are inherently bad; therefore, there is no need, nor necessity, nor should they be cooperative unless it furthers their objectives. They know that there is no need to cooperate, and that they must not give up on their objectives because the serfs at the bottom class are inherently not good. Because they are not good, they are free to treat these people as deplorables and they have no ethical responsibilities to them except to give them a minimum standard of living and no more.

H. Ok.

D. And, because they know the other person to be of an inherently bad nature, they know that control is preferable to cooperative behavior. The Leftist knows that there should not be a need to be cooperative and only their priorities are of importance in the dissemination of the rules, regulations, and laws of society. As this viewpoint becomes more and more prevalent within their minds and purview of perception, Dictum 5, the Lord Acton Principle, takes over, and their minds become corrupted in that they can only think of their own priorities, and thus, cooperative abilities diminish. When cooperative abilities diminish, then only their objectives remain. When only their objectives remain, respect is no longer needed with the other person because only control is needed to force the other person to work to obtain the objectives of the Haves. Examples of this are Kings and Queens throughout history, Stalin, Mao, Hitler and really almost any political action of the Haves when dealing with the Have-Nots.

H. Could you make that a little bit simpler to understand?

D. Yes. The primary principle involved is that of ethics. Ethics is the appropriate dispensation of respect. Respect is the evolutionary mechanism by which we are able to cooperate because it reduces aggression and gives signs to the other that we are willing to cooperate. We cooperate in order to produce goods and services more efficiently. We produce goods and services to bring us up away from misery, which is the essence of good.

H. Yes, I remember.

D. It's this appropriate dispensation of respect that is applicable in commercial and social situations.

H. An example of a commercial situation would be our respect for our boss, the president of the company, and the people we work

47

with, all of whom we need in order to cooperatively produce whatever good or service that we are working on. In a social situation, we would give respect to our parents who bring us up; and, naturally, we want to cooperate with them because we are grateful for their indulgence, giving us so much of their effort in raising us to be adults. We give respect to them because they have been good to us, and they want the best for us.

D. The next principle that comes into play is the Lord Acton Principle which says that power tends to corrupt, and absolute power corrupts absolutely. And, this happens because as a person becomes more and more powerful, it really means that he has more and more control over those around him and below him in the sense that he no longer needs to cooperate with them. And, the more he doesn't need to cooperate with them, the more he may consider his own priorities in life which he uses to make decisions. When we make a cooperative decision, there are two parts to the decision. The first part is our own decision to cooperate to produce something, and the other part is the other person's decision to cooperate with us. Each party in a cooperative situation establishes its priorities and then effectuates those priorities, which by the way, as we have already pointed out, is the nature of freedom.

H. Yes, to reiterate, freedom is the establishment of our priorities and then the effectuation of our priorities. When during the day the pangs of hunger start pinging on our consciousness, we make a priority which is a piece of knowledge that we are hungry, and we decide to do something about it. Our making a meal and then eating it is the effectuation of that priority to satisfy the hunger which was the establishment of the priority. These actions together represent freedom.

D. So, in a cooperative commercial situation, each party to the agreement uses their freedom to establish the priority and effectuates it by working together to produce something. If one inhabitant of the cooperative agreement gains more control over the situation, his priorities become salient and prevalent within the cooperative agreement, lessening the essence and the power of the agreement. The powerful or controlling party will make its priorities, and, as such, they begin to replace the priorities of the others within the agreement, thereby demeaning the priorities of others and the meaning of the essence of the cooperative agreement. Adding to this process of control affecting the compact or cooperative agreement is the corruption that is spoken about in Lord Acton's famous expression. And thus, the priorities, as they become created by one person only, fulfill the concept of corruption.

H. OK, very interesting.

D. When one's priorities become all prevailing within the agreement, cooperative respect goes to zero, and the one party with all the control relies on their own priorities totally; and when it becomes total, then it is absolute corruption because of the absolute power as the cooperative agreements have disappeared and are replaced by the priorities of one party only.

H. OK, so I see now how absolute power corrupts absolutely. But, how does this affect the situation of the use of ethics in the lives of either cooperative participants in a social or commercial agreement or for that one person who becomes corrupted completely and becomes a complete controller of others? What is the connection; what is the segue?

D. All we need to do now is to go back and review the ingredients of that which is ethical and the connection will become clear.

H. OK, as I wrote the book on it, I can enumerate those ingredients. Ethics is the dispensation of respect; we respect others when we consider them important to us; they are important to us because they help us produce goods and services in a commercial situation; and in a social situation, respect helps us with our daily lives allowing us to live with others in harmony. As such, commercially and socially, cooperative actions produce goodness and goodness brings us up away from misery; therefore, it is good to be ethical.

D. Exactly. The more something is important to us, the more we respect it. And the reverse is true. Therefore, the less we respect somebody, it is because we realize that they are producing less good through cooperative action. When the mind becomes corrupt in the one who controls everything, he no longer has to cooperate with anybody but just initiates his priorities. Therefore, the powerful person who controls others will have little or even no respect for others because they are no longer important inside a cooperative agreement; and if they have no respect for them, ethics is no longer a consideration because ethics is the appropriate dispensation of respect. Those who are controlled will fall into that serf, proletariat, or slave category.

H. And as such, there would be little or no respect going to the lower classes such as slaves and those very close to being slaves. We can see, throughout history, that being the case for sure. Even in modern-day television, we have seen politicians refer to people of the working class as the "deplorables."

D. History shows us that the royal class always looks down on the working class, or slaves, as we have just shown why. If respect is

50

not needed, then ethics in that relationship is nonexistent.

H. So ethics, necessarily, cannot be part of the upper control class' relationship with the lower proletariat, working, and slavery classes. If there is no respect, then there will be a tendency to treat them badly.

D. That's right.

H. My gosh, we certainly have numerous examples throughout history of the royal class using the lower classes as chattel or slaughtering the lower classes for the fulfillment of any of one or several ideologies, a few of which have already been enumerated.

D. So, when the royal class does not have an ethical standard by which they know how they should behave, then that what remains is the end justifies the means.

H. Amazingly, the utilitarian slogan of the end justifies the means is really the lack of ethics.

D. Not only is it the lack of ethics, but it is also the total corruption of one's mind when one person has no respect for others in human society. Even by just being human, another person deserves a modicum of respect and, therefore, is due ethical behavior. Therefore, those of the class of the Haves have no nadir for the lack of respect that they may show to others outside of the royal class.

H. It's interesting that you say that. Looking back throughout history, the royal stratum, of course, has had little regard for the lower classes such as the slaves, the proletariat, and the working classes, and this is akin to the way the Leftist-Haves look down upon those of the lower Have-Not classes. Thus, the aristocracies throughout the world realized that you can only take the lower classes so far before they will revolt and come after you. The absolute rule of the royal Have class produces governments that strive toward disarming the peasant Have-Not class. Societies throughout the world and throughout history have tried to ban the lower classes from having any sort of weapons at all. Governments throughout the world even try to ban certain types of knives. And, why shouldn't they? Revolutions happen.

D. And this leads us again to the seventh Dictum which is that the Haves always seek more control of others (the Have-Nots) while enjoying freedom for themselves.

H. So, let's get back to the principles of the Have-Nots. I know we have already talked about Dictum 3, but what does it mean to be a conservative and a person of the Right? As a matter of fact, it's probably pretty important to define it, because you often hear the expression by the Leftist about the "extreme Right." It seems pretty clear they want to tell you how terrible is somebody of the extreme Right. Professor, what is somebody on the extreme Right, and what is the essence of somebody who is a conservative? What are those principles that govern the political class of the Right? Are the Have-Nots synonymous with the conservative Right?

D. Well, as mentioned, there are also seven principles pertaining to the Have-Not Conservative, and the first two are the same as the Left. Dictums 1 and 2 are exactly the same, as these principles exist all throughout human nature, throughout all peoples of the earth. When it comes to Dictum 3, there's a difference that we have already discussed a little bit ago. Dictum 3 says that those, who are conservative, look to the other person as essentially having a good nature.

H. Yes, we have already mentioned that.

D. The fourth Dictum is the duty of sustaining freedom for the individual which replaces Noblesse Oblige of the Haves, and Dictum 5 indicates that freedom begets ethicalities absolutely and within ethics is the will to cooperate through respect which dictates that charity should be voluntary. Thus, the Have-Nots believe that there should be no compulsion in creating a social net. They believe that it should be voluntary charity.

H. The problem with this is that the Leftist-Haves do not believe in voluntary charity because the social net cannot be constructed to the degree that they need in order to be able to manage and control society sufficiently so that they'll be no revenge upon them (the Haves) even if they do confiscate all the weapons. And this brings me to an interesting question: can voluntary charity replace a Have governmentally-driven social net to provide for the destitute, less fortunate Have-Nots in society?

D. As we noted, the Have-Nots are generally people who have a good view of the nature of their societal companions, while the Haves think that the others in society are not inherently good. As far as I can estimate, people are born this way and society has about 30% of each category. Then, there are the independents who don't think about human nature as either good or bad, and that's about 40% of the populace.

H. Well, that makes sense because it seems that no matter how unpopular a president becomes, his polling popularity does not seem to break below the 30% mark. That said, the Have-Nots, who hold to Dictum 3, will see no reason to have a social net as they are coming out of the lower class and will want to jump out and up into the middle class for a better life, fulfilling Dictum 1.

Of course, there will be some in the lower classes that are accustomed to the guaranteed life as provided by the noble class, and as such, will not have the motivation to jump out into the middle class and will keep their situation of being in the lower class, especially if they're getting welfare; it's enough to live on, if they are not well motivated. But, for those who are highly motivated by Dictums 1 and 2, they will be predisposed to strive, work hard, and come out of the proletariat class and get into the middle class by the use of their knowledge and effort. At least three Dicta of life - wanting that which is good for it; that life is imbued with the principle of Libido Dominandi and from that there evolved the will to compete; that others have a good nature - will fulfill the core beliefs of the Have-Nots which are people of a conservative mindset who form the basis of the Republican party and its policies dating all the way back to its inception with Abraham Lincoln and even before to the Founding Fathers.

H. Sure, I can understand that. Abraham Lincoln, naturally, was of the Republican party which was the party of preventing the expansion of slavery. Have-Nots would construct such a party of anti-slavery because the Have-Nots came out of the lower classes, and all these Have-Nots tried to come up into the middle class and do well for themselves. They recognized the strife and struggle needed to bring goodness to oneself, and it's a natural thing to conclude that everybody should have a right to come out of the lower classes.

D. Good observation.

H. So, let's continue to answer the question about whether or not voluntary charity is sufficient to establish a social net.

D. It is sufficient for the Have-Nots and insufficient for the Haves.

It is insufficient for the Haves because they need to prevent a people's revolution whereby there would be an insurrection of the slaves or the proletariats which could overthrow the Haves. So, they are desirous of a fully-funded system, whereby they can provide a reasonable subsistence level to the slaves and the proletariats, to ensure that the Haves can supply the Have-Nots with a minimum safety net. In order to effectuate this, they need a fully-funded program, and they need full control of it.

H. What is control again?

D. Control is the usurpation of freedom by an outside source. It is essentially the forced substitution of another's priorities and subsequently the effectuation of the new priority of the outside source. The control can be either partial or complete.

D. So, the Haves by their nature (consisting of Haves-Dicta 1, 2, 3, 4, 5, 6), in every case, want to increase control in society, and they do this by substituting their priorities for your priorities, or the priorities of other individuals within society, perforce, as force is a necessary condition for the Haves, because without it, individuals as per Dictums 1 and 2 are not going to necessarily allow other individuals to come into their own lives and replace their own priorities with the priorities of somebody else.

H. Control being anathema to the Have-Nots, the only way the Have-Nots could accept the priorities of somebody else is through intellectual debate.

D. That's right! That's the nature of our conflict in life.

H. What!? I could then readily conclude from that statement that all conflict in society is from the problem of forceful control of others.

D. Yes.

H. So, in this case, we are looking at the problem of charity versus a state-run social net. Which is better? How does society answer this question? How does a society choose which system to go for? And we have to decide this in the context of what we just concluded, which is that control breeds conflict!

D. Right. Let's see if we can answer this question. The first characteristic we need to understand is that the Haves need to place within society a social net that fulfills their Noblesse Oblige contractual arrangement with society, and they need to do this to protect themselves from the masses. The Have-Nots have to go to work every day to fulfill the requirements of the Haves in the production of products and services for the society of the Haves. It is by its nature selfish.

H. Selfish? That's like saying all those who are Leftists or Democrats or Socialists are selfish? But I don't think that they are. At least my impression is that they sincerely want a base social net for the poor of the world.

D. It is selfish because it fulfills the nature of control. They want to implement their priority of a social welfare program that is for their benefit and not really for the benefit of the poor as per their ideology of Noblesse Oblige, Dictum 4. It is implanted in society to perpetuate the society of the Haves. It limits the freedom of the Have-Nots in society because it appropriates the goods and services produced by the workers of society to be taken away and used for the parasitic Haves with a portion of it to be used for those Have-Nots that are poor and not prospering in society.

H. Well, at least one aspect of it shows that it is a noble cause because they are, at least, partially providing for the poor of society.

D. There is an element of veracity here. The idea of a social network for the poor of society is by itself a good thought. But so is the thought that people will be generous enough in charity to provide for the same thing. It's a question of which is more efficient and which is better for society. The thought remains in the consideration of the Have-Nots.

H. But as you mentioned, the Haves use control which has the ingredient to force upon the Have-Not individuals of society the priorities of the Haves. It would seem to me that within this action of force, we have an ethical component within it making it sound aesthetically pleasing to a society. What do you think, Professor?

D. To answer this question about which is better for society: whether significant control by government-funded programs to establish a social net or whether voluntary charity is more efficient and is better for society to establish a social net for the poor, we again have to recall both the philosopher William James and the physicist Albert Einstein in order to understand the truth in the answer.

H. Yes, I remember from my third book, *Truth and the Nature of Decisions.* William James said that truth is that which can be corroborated and verified; and Einstein demonstrated that everything requires a point of reference.

D. From an individual's ethical point of view, it is unethical for one individual to dominate another person by controlling the other's priorities, preventing one's ability to create a priority in one's consciousness and effectuate it by an action that we know as freedom. We know this because of the nature of ethics. On the one side of the ethical ledger, we have the Left indicating that to

57

provide a sufficient social net we need the assistance of a government-funded program; and this is would be ethical if the democratic republic constituency voted it in as a policy to be implemented by their government facilitators and representatives. If they vote in a bunch of Leftist-Haves that would want a totally funded government program to establish the welfare of society as per Dictum 4, then so be it. It is their right within the rules set up by the contract with their government. In the U.S., it's noted as the Constitution, of course.

H. So, it is a question for a democracy within a republic to settle. I think de Tocqueville pointed this out when he said that the majority can run tyranny over the minority. I see his point! It's a matter of perspective in seeking truth.

D. Of course, underlying this problem is the thought that government programs are notoriously inefficient. As far as I can figure, it's about a 1 to 9 ratio of government inefficiency compared to the private initiative of efficiencies in organizations whereby it basically is the reverse of the inefficiency of governmental institutions. In other words, a charitable or private corporate efficiency can be as efficient as 9 to 1. So, if you donate $10 to a charitable organization in order to effectuate a service, $1 would go to the organization for facilitating the service and $9 to the beneficiaries of the service. In a governmental organization, it is probably about 90% of the funds to the government and 10% to the social net, but perhaps I am being prejudicial in my assessment. Be that as it may be, the individual societies throughout the world have to decide democratically whether to place their need for services within the government or within private or charitable organizations.

H. I expect that those percentages are approximately true, but of course, research would have to be done to understand it more precisely. But suffice it to say that if we generally take a look at the nations throughout the world that effectuate all social services, those that have the government do more would not be as wealthy and their societal population would be poor. If we take a look at North Korea where everything is government controlled, the populace is as poor as church mice. Same would be true for other such societies such as Cuba or Venezuela. The more control the government exerts over its populace and the more it decides and controls society, the poorer is that country. And not only is it poor, but its government is also brutal.

D. Oh excellent point! And the brutality comes from the institution of control. As freedom dissipates and the amount that governmental institutions interrupt the creation of priorities by individuals proliferates, the more the individuals become upset because it contradicts the First Dictum of Life: all of life seeks that which is good for it, and it seeks what is good for it by instituting its own priorities, then effectuating those priorities which is, as we have noted, the essence of freedom.

H. So, it is, as we see around the world, that the wealthier societies are the ones that have the least amount of control over the constituent individuals of that nation's society.

D. It is a truism that the more freedom, the greater the wealth of the nation, and the better and the happier the lower classes of society would be. So, a possible rational and pragmatic solution to this problem, whereby you have to decide whether the social net should be effectuated by the government or by private charity, would be an admixture of employing both the government and private charities. There would be both governmental and private budgets to be established for the granting of services to the poor.

The government would donate to charity to effectuate the welfare services an amount, in addition to the private amount that these charities need, that would be sufficient to effectuate the level of service that is mandated by society and by Dictum 4 of the Have-Nots. That way there would be the employment of the efficiency of the private organization as well as the minimum funding which would be guaranteed by governmental funding.

H. So now, the obvious question is why is it that control breeds inefficiency in the production of goods and services? And really, we can extrapolate that question out to be why is our government inherently less efficient than private corporations. Is there something in the principles, that you have elucidated, that dictates this phenomenon?

D. It is control: the more control that a governmental institution employs, the less efficient a society becomes. The reason for this is that the production of knowledge becomes controlled and ultimately decreases as control increases. In other words, control lessens the amount of knowledge within society and decreases its productivity efficiencies in the production of goods and services.

H. Why is this?

D. This is because freedom is decreased. When freedom is decreased, that means the priorities, that are constructed and then effectuated by the various individuals in society, are decreased because the private production of priorities is substituted with the priorities of a governmental institution. Priorities are pieces of knowledge, and if you decrease knowledge within society, it necessarily becomes less efficient.

H. Yes, I remember this from our discussion in *The Philosophical Equations of Economics.* Knowledge is the chief progenitor of goods and services because, in a modern advanced society, most of the goods and services are chiefly made up of knowledge. Secondly, we may further add that the concentration of production of knowledge in one entity does not have the overall brain power of the production of knowledge that can exist using the entire population of a society. The brain power of the government is nothing compared to the brain power en masse of the populace and the citizens of society.

D. And there's a secondary reason also. When a priority is generated by a control center, such as a governmental institution, the priority could be very different from the priorities generated by the poor who are the ones to receive the social net benefits. The priorities of the Haves are often very different from the priorities of the Have-Nots. An example would be whereby the Haves want to give out largess, benefits, and welfare in exchange for receiving the votes of these constituents. The bourgeois Have-Nots on the other hand would want to give out benefits in order to give the beneficiaries time to re-establish or educate themselves so that they can get another job and get off of the welfare dole and become productive members of society so that the working tax paying Have-Nots do not continue to pay for the non-working Have-Nots.

H. Well, that's an interesting point of view between the different perspectives of the Leftist-Haves and the Have-Not-Right. I'm sure there are other differences. Let's, Professor, continue examining the differences between the Haves and the Have-Nots.

D. The division starts, as we spoke before, with the advent of a leader within society caused by Dictums 1 and 2. As soon as there appears someone within society with more power than the others, that means there's a discrepancy in the amount of goods and services that one controls more than another in society.

H. You're speaking of the control which governmental society would possess. In other words, in referring to those with higher societal responsibilities which we will call "government," this is different from the Have-Nots of society which is composed of the proletariats, the workers, the slaves, the serfs.

D. The second discrepancy within society is caused by the differentiation of the individuals which results in various degrees of creativity, amounts, and types of the production of goods and services. Individuals often have their various niches in which one is better than another thus giving total differentiation to society as a whole.

H. Yes, I remember this is the Law of Differentiation as we discussed in my fourth book, *The Philosophical Equations of Economics.*

D. Because of this differentiation, one individual may produce or create a new invention bringing in an efficiency into society and consequently giving him the opportunity to create wealth in society. This wealth creation is the result of the efficiencies, and it causes a differentiation in wealth of, and in output by, one individual over another.

H. Yes, I remember. And the new production will find its own demand because of Dictum 1. Once the new supplier realizes that there will be a demand for his product or service, the buyer could make payment by also inventing various types of services or products and offering to swap and trade with the new supplier through products, or in money, that a person who demands that product can come up with. In a rudimentary society, let's say somebody comes up with a better way to hunt, such as, with a bow and arrow. Once that's invented through the division of labor, payment can be made to other members of society for receiving the bow and arrow by supplying different services, such as by helping out the producer with new services of their own for the family.

D. Correct, there are two differentials that create efficiencies in society. One is the improvement of a product or service that brings an efficiency, and the other one is the rise of a political leader because he produces an efficiency in how society runs as a whole. On top of this, we must add Saint Augustine's principle of Libido Dominandi which causes the essence of political division to emerge which is the Haves versus the Have-Nots.

H. So society evolved from this very beginning where there are two classes which are the Haves and the Have-Nots. And they are, as I understand it, the two basic political divisions in politics.

D. The evolutionary lineage of the Have-Nots is fairly simple. There are the workers of society and they come from nothing. They would like to fulfill Dictum 1 that living entities go about their lives doing what they need to do in order to live. But as per most of the history of societies, the Have-Nots never had much. They never had any land because that was always owned by the Haves.

H. Right.

D. So, the essence of the Have-Nots is that they are the worker bees of society. They are the proletariats, the serfs, the working class, and the slaves. And the only difference between a slave, a serf, or a proletariat is the amount of control that has been exerted over these individuals by the Haves. Arbitrarily, we could denote percentages as if they were a tax. Complete control, i.e., 100%

would mean slavery; 90% control would mean a serf and servant; 80% would mean a prole; and 50% someone of the upper lower class, such as a merchant or someone of a service guild.

H. Exactly, the amount of control indicates what class that one is in society. Slaves, of course, would be the bottom class, and just up from there would be the serfs and the farmers and all the others that receive much of the control that the Haves have dished out. And as with all life entities, the Haves and the Have-Nots are subject to Dictum 1, since both classes seek that which is good for them.

D. And some of the things that are good for them are the other basic concepts that all seek for themselves such as peace, justice, fairness, a better life for oneself, and a higher standard of living. When these denizens of society are allowed to seek that which is good for them, they're automatically at peace with themselves because they are left alone fulfilling their primary objective in life which is to seek goodness and continually seek goodness, in their lives, Dictum 1. And I say that because when one first obtains goodness, it's not enough. All life continually seeks goodness and more and more goodness and wants to do so with equality before the law so that opportunity is uniform and equitable for all society's denizens.

H. But the Left would raise a contrarian point of view in saying that being equal before the law does not guarantee an equitable opportunity within society and that is immoral, unjust, and unconscionable. They often accuse people who have more as having privilege and specifically white privilege. But I wonder what is the meaning of privilege, or white privilege as they are want to point out, or any kind of privilege for that matter.

D. Privilege means one person receives one or more rights more than another person, and so, it could be said that this is unfair; and it is true, and it is un-American, and it is against the intent and purpose of the U.S. Constitution. It existed certainly in the past in Europe as there existed feudal societies that had the basic Haves and Have-Nots type of society throughout its history. These European societies with their royalties did produce classes of privilege. The Haves of royalty had privilege. They had rights that the lower classes did not have. An example of this would be the Roman Patricians who had rights not available to the Plebians, the Freeman, and the Slaves.

H. Does American society not have the privileged class that critics proclaim we have? Do not some have big beautiful houses, go to private clubs, send their children to the best private college preparatory schools, then to the best universities, and so on?

D. Certainly people of greater economic means do so, but they do so through their greater pecuniary means, not because they are privileged.

H. OK, privilege means to possess a right that another person does not, and in this case, the one person has a financial means greater than another, and thus, that person would have at least the economic right to greater privilege.

D. On the contrary, the privilege does not exist since the extraordinary right does not exist because a right can only exist if there is a corresponding obligation.

H. Really?

D. Rights and obligations exist only within contracts, covenants, or agreements. In any cooperative agreement, there are two or more parties who exclaim that they are willing to exchange their labor or products. In doing so, each party will have a right to receive something and an obligation to give something.

H. Yes, I understand. If I am at the store buying something, I have the obligation to give the checkout clerk the money for the cost of the item that I wish to buy, and I have the right to receive that item. The store clerk also has a right to receive my money for the item along with the obligation to give me the item.

D. In European royalty societies of old, sometimes the Haves would unilaterally arrogate rights unto themselves without the corresponding obligation; such as the right to enter an exclusive institution of higher education without the corresponding obligation to pay for it and without the need (or obligation) to work extra hard and pass competitive tests that would indicate superior intellectual achievement and thus deserve to be admitted. In past societies that had slaves in service, there was the unilateral right to receive the labor of a man (the slave) without the obligation of having to pay for it as slaves were chattel and not an entity with which a person needed to create an agreement in order to work together. In present American society, there is no such legal situation. Our laws prevent the establishment of rights without the corresponding obligation.

H. I see. So, in theory, the wealthy person joining an exclusive club or sending his progeny to an expensive school does so because he can fulfill his obligation to pay for it and the child can demonstrate intellectual superiority. The well-off people of American society have accumulated wealth completely from cooperative situations (excepting of course the criminal), thereby fulfilling their economic rights and obligations, and as such, a generic American societal white privilege does not exist. It can only be in individual cases where the right exists without the corresponding obligation.

D. Correct.

H. The Have-Nots are seeking and striving for life, liberty, and the pursuit of happiness as stated in the Declaration of Independence and similarly stated in the Bill of Rights which is the essence of being a conservative and being on the Right side of the political equation, or I should say, the political spectrum. Of course, they are subject to the seven principles that we've already outlined here today, and it seems to be simple and straightforward. They haven't much, and all they seek is that which is good for them.

D. That's right! On the other side of the political spectrum are the Haves, and they are more complicated. Let's go over the hierarchy. As we said before, it certainly starts with the person who has control; thus, it would be the king and queen. Then, underneath them are the nobles or other royalty who are needed to facilitate the wishes, regulations, and edicts that the king and queen produce. Next in line would be those who work for the nobles which we've already deemed to be the facilitators which would be the government bureaucracy and the corporate executives who carry out the wishes of the nobles and indirectly the king and queen.

H. And these upper classes oppress the lower classes!

D. Because of Dictum 5 which is the Lord Acton Principle that power corrupts and absolute power corrupts absolutely, we know that the treatment of the lower classes tends to get worse. The royalty tends to look down on the lower classes as something to control. And as their attitude tends to become more corrupt due to their ability to garner and accumulate more control of the lower classes, their attitude diminishes and degrades, and they look at the lower classes as just something to be controlled and utilized for their own purposes.

H. That's right, all we have to do is look at history for confirmation of this attitude. All you have to note is the amount of slaughter that the Haves have committed upon the Have-Nots in the various ways that history has exhibited, such as by sending them to war or collectivizing them and sending them to concentration-work camps. Throughout history, they care little about the Have-Nots. They are just something to be used for their own purposes (that is, the king and queen and the nobles) which is to accumulate more goodness for themselves, such as conquering other nations in order to instill their ideology or other desiderata upon others. The Haves have no end to their avariciousness, and we can say this because all life seeks that which is good for it and continually seeks that which is good for it.

D. Well said. But at some point, history has indicated that the downtrodden become so disheartened that they rebel, even if they have no weapons. Because they have no hope in life having no chance to fulfill Dictum 1, they rebel.

H. Yes, this is as exhibited by the French revolutions and others previously. I assume therefore at this point that we are to invoke Dictum 4 which is Noblesse Oblige which is control through contract. The nobles formulate the idea that they will provide a certain level of living in exchange for the loyalty of the lower classes to governmental control by the Haves.

D. But at this point there are some within the lower classes that don't want to be in the lower classes and want to become fulfilled as per Dictum 1 that all life wants to seek more of what is good for them. There are some that do not want to submit to the control of the Haves and do not want to continue to serve them, be a slave, or be a worker bee for the Haves. There are those Have-Nots that want to break out of the social network of serfdom, and it will be thought and considered by the Haves that these non-cooperative denizens of serfdom that adhere to individual rights are basically bad people and that their nature is inherently bad. Further, because they are bad, there is no respect for the individual rights of these Have-Nots whether they are conformists (those that stay in their lower class) or non-conformists (those that attempt to break out of their lower class). In the eyes of the Rightly-Guided Haves, they are inherently bad people that need to be controlled (Dictum 3). And so, controlled they must be.

Chapter 3 - Control & Knowledge

H. And control is negative knowledge plus force.

D. And the purpose of this control is to subdue the Have-Nots so they don't rise out of their lower class. This necessary control means that there will be economic and equal social justice for the Have-Nots whereby everybody stays where they are in society, whereby everybody is equal in every way. And because they are bad, there is no empathy for the advocate of individual rights of the Have-Nots.

H. Yes, I can see that this is true. And in some of their political speeches, they confirmed this with the verbiage that they use, as some of the Haves of the political class actually call those of the Have-Nots, "the deplorables."

D. And so the Rightly-Guided Haves try to construct caste fascism or caste socialism. In modern-day democracies, for example, the society progresses and becomes more complicated, and as such, the size of the nobles and their associates become ever and ever larger. These associate groups are the bureaucrats and corporate management. These groups are needed in order to control the Have-Nots as their numbers have enlarged, and correspondingly, so has the amount of edicts, laws, and regulations that the Haves need to generate in order to control society and the Have-Nots.

H. And why these corporate executives?

D. Corporate management is needed because they control a large number of workers who are of the lower classes and a large number of employees of the middle class. As such, the Haves have recognized the efficacy of incorporating them into the facilitator class of the Haves who are controlled by the upper level of the facilitator class which is the higher level of the government bureaucracy that is the replacement for the erstwhile noble class which is subject to the political class historically which in times of yore was known as the king and queen.

H. So, the essence of it all is an hierarchy of control of the several classes each one dominating the other; and all this in accordance with Dictum 1 (all life does that which is good for it and continually does that which is good for it) and Dictum 2 (Libido Dominandi).

D. Correct.

H. So, it seems that control is the distinguishing factor that segregates the various classes. Let's review the essence of control.

D. Control is anti-cooperative. It is the supplanting by force the priorities of one person using instead the priorities of the another.

H. What is cooperation?

D. Cooperation equals time, the energy to produce its intended result, plus the knowledge that the cooperative time and effort will result in achieving more of the desiderata that will occur when more than one gather to produce something than if one were to do it alone which is, in essence, an agreement with another (or others).

H. Yes, and as I previously explained in *The Nature of Ethics: Defining Ethics, Good and Evil*, we cooperate through the use of

71

respect as the evolutionary trait that alleviates aggressive behavior, and we respect others because we consider them important, and we consider others important when they are instrumental in producing something of value such as a good or a service that consists of goodness, and that which is good brings us up away from misery.

D. Excellent!

H. So, you mentioned that control is anti-cooperative behavior.

D. It is composed of the knowledge of all the laws, regulations, edicts that emanate from the Rightly-Guided Haves that prevent freedom which is the construction of priorities and the actuation of those priorities; and thus, we can say that control is negative knowledge plus force.

H. And as we have established, freedom is the creation of priorities and the activation of those priorities and those priorities are the desiderata of our lives.

D. Additionally, it should be noted that priorities are, essentially, bytes of knowledge, and thus, the laws, regulations, and edicts of the Haves are for the most part negative knowledge, or in other words, anti-knowledge.

H. What is negative knowledge?

D. The elements of negative knowledge are the laws, regulations, and edicts of the Haves that detract from the efficiency of the production of our desiderata and from the production of goods and services.

H. OK, I can see that this is possible, as anti-knowledge equals those priorities that detract from the efficiency of the production of our desiderata making our lives and our economy less efficient. Of course, I understand that there are some rules and regulations that actually can make an economy ultimately more efficient. Examples of this would be the laws that set up a judicial system that would assist a society to settle disputes, questions of contracts, or adjudicating the criminal system; the laws that govern the administration of a police system so that societal order is maintained; the regulations of administering environmental laws, and so on.

D. When these laws and regulations make society more efficient, they become positive knowledge; and when they make society inefficient, they become anti-knowledge, or negative knowledge, and they can be expressed and inserted into our philosophical equation of the economic transaction.

H. As I transcribed this basic equation in the *Philosophical Equations of Economics*, every economic transaction can be described as a sacrifice versus a reward with the variables being risk (as a percentage), information/knowledge (in bytes), time (in seconds), and effort (in ergs) for a service; and if the transaction involves a product or good, then we would add in material (in grams to represent mass), or land as the economists would say. And so the negative knowledge component could be added as a subtraction of the information/knowledge variable of the equation and the basic equation would be the Sacrifice equals the Reward which would have the variables:

$$Sacrifice = (R_{\%})(K/I_{bytes})(T_{sec})(E_{ergs})(M_g) = Reward = (R_{\%})(K/I_{bytes})(T_{sec})(E_{ergs})(M_g)$$

D. And this transactional equation is the effectuation portion of

73

freedom.

Author's note: for a complete discussion of this equation see *The Philosophical Equations of Economics* by this author. Please note that the variables are multiplied together instead of added as multiplication allows the result to be consistent with dimensional analysis and is not meant to represent how the cerebral mind works in making a decision. The process of addition would make the equation incongruent due to dimensional analysis.

H. Please explain further.

D. Freedom is multi-dimensional. The first dimension is the incoming stimuli of which there are two types: interior originating stimuli and exterior originating stimuli.

H. I remember. The interior originating stimuli are experiences that come from inside the body to the consciousness and the exterior originating stimuli come from without.

D. The existence of the stimuli in the living entity's consciousness is the first dimension thus formulating the existence of knowledge in the consciousness. The second dimension is the degree, or intensity, of the incoming stimuli, should the information contained inside the knowledge increase. The third dimension of the knowledge is the time of the knowledge that will be required should the individual activate and effectuate the priority which is followed by the effort, or energy, that will be necessary to institute the priority which is an integral part of the knowledge. Lastly, there is the risk/opportunity percentage component of the knowledge indicating how much danger or risk there is in the effectuation or how much opportunity there is in its initiation. Of course, if the intended effectuation of the priority is a material thing, then we add the mass component to the equation.

H. Please summarize.

D. The creation of the priority is composed of the stimuli at the consciousness which represents the creation of a piece of knowledge when an importance is attached to it. Then these other components of the piece of knowledge are added making the priority complete, ready to be effectuated. These components of a priority are gathered within the consciousness, then the intellectual faculties of the life entity take over to make the decision whether to effectuate or not.

H. Maybe we should review the difference between information and knowledge. I got the impression from what you just said that they are synonymous, but from our previous discussion, I believe that they are not.

D. Information is a component of knowledge. It is the raw stimuli that come to the consciousness, then in order to be upgraded to the knowledge level, the consciousness needs to add in the component of importance to the piece of information. Without the notion of importance, we will not retain it in memory for long. However, when the importance of the incoming stimuli is accredited by the consciousness to the information, this importance causes the information to jump to the status of knowledge; and because all bytes of knowledge have an importance component to it, the byte of knowledge is equivalent to a priority.

H. So, all of our knowledge that is remembered and used by us humans is prioritized?

D. Yes, we retain knowledge because it is important to us. The more a piece of knowledge is deemed to be important, the more we will attempt to remember and employ that piece of knowledge. Information, on the other hand, does not have any importance attached to it and therefore is usually (but not necessarily) soon forgotten unless it is stored away in an exterior memory or sub-memory. Thus, informational stimuli are not retained as much. If it has the potential to have some sort of importance in the future, it will be stored in a computer or by some other method such as in a book or on a piece of paper until a priority is attached to the information making it a piece of knowledge.

H. Then, may I conclude that informational importance equals knowledge?

D. Yes, information plus importance equals knowledge.

H. Would you be able to define importance for me? It seems to me that an importance would be a piece of knowledge itself.

D. It is the precursor to knowledge. Interior or exterior originating stimuli that ping our consciousness are required. Once pinged, the life energy, that makes us animate and that distinguishes life from the inanimate, assigns to the information an importance, and as such, the informational stimuli become useful knowledge; and the more important it is, the more we are apt to remember and employ it in our lives.

H. It is as if the life force of the consciousness receives the incoming informational stimuli generating qualitative importance which is attached to the byte of information that produces a new piece of compound information which would be knowledge.

D. One way we could symbolize this is to say that information times the newly conscious life force generates a piece of importance which when it exceeds a certain internally understood level of importance equals the new byte of knowledge which is a priority; and thus, where I equals information in bytes and L equals the life force generated piece of importance, we have:

$$(I_{bytes})(L_{ergs}) = K_{byte\text{-}ergs}$$

H. That's interesting! Knowledge is composed of bytes of information plus a quantity of life energy! Therefore, knowledge is a form of energy!

D. Yes, we have to establish our new advanced equation for the transaction indicating how human beings operate. So, we will take our newfound understanding of knowledge which is now byte-ergs and will substitute that into the equation. Consequently, we can now say:

$$Sacrifice\ (R_{(\%)}I/K_{(byte\text{-}ergs)}T_{(sec)}E_{(ergs)}M_{(mass)}) = Rwd\ (R_{(\%)}I/K_{(byte\text{-}ergs)}T_{(sec)}E_{(ergs)}M_{(mass)})$$

H. Ok.

D. This discovery that knowledge is a form of energy will allow us to make some new conclusions. Previously, we indicated that the difference between information and knowledge is that knowledge is information plus a priority. But there actually is a problem with this. It means that there was a piece of knowledge out there that didn't have an antecedent of information. This is because information, that is going to become knowledge, has to be bonded with a piece of knowledge that is a priority in order to become knowledge. Therefore, as we just said, this situation would pre-date all information that comes to us as knowledge.

H. Yes right!

D. We could rationalize how this is possible by understanding that genetics precedes our ability to intake information coming from both outside the body and inside the body to our consciousness. This genetic information would hold the priorities that give the life entity the ability to raise the status of the information, which the life entity is already holding and possessing, to the status of being a priority. Genetic information comes with the priority already attached to it. And, if it's genetic in nature, it is, ipso facto, part of the life force that is within the life entity, and thus, genetic information should actually be noted as genetic knowledge. Therefore, this needs to be noted in our equation.

H. Convenient! But it is essential for us to be consistent. And, it also helps to further, more assuredly, explain, that which was noted in my third book, *Truth and the Nature of Decisions*, the proof for the existence of God.

D. Please review that for us.

H. In order for a life entity to come into being, it requires that molecules, or compound molecules, go from an inanimate state to an animate state, to enable the life entity to perform the work necessary for the life entity to exist, and allow the life entity to make decisions. In order for a molecule to make a decision, it requires knowledge. Knowledge must be attached to the molecule in order for it to operate as a life entity. This means that knowledge pre-existed the molecule, and of course, we must search for the origin of that knowledge. Invoking the arguments of philosophers, such as Aquinas, whereby we search backward to the origin of life, we come to the primal source which they and we conclude is God.

D. And now, we come to the understanding that knowledge itself has the life force attached to it and is in its essence animate and of life; and so now, it's possible to justify and validate this argument for the existence of God.

H. It seems like we have wandered far afield in our conversation.

D. Not really. Our purpose here is to define control and discover its relationship to the concept of freedom as we will remember that control is a direct and overwhelming objective for the Haves.

H. Right. Control is needed by the Haves to keep the Have-Nots in their class and to prevent them from jumping into the middle class. And of course, additionally, the Haves must gain control of the emerging prosperous middle class in order to prevent them from jumping further upward entering and being of the facilitator class; or even more anathema yet, to prevent them actually jumping into the exclusivity of the governance and royalty class preserving the integrity of Dicta 4, 6, and 7 of the Haves.

D. So, let's review and summarize the relevant definitions of the concepts that we're discussing. First, freedom is the construction and then the effectuation of one's priorities. Anti-freedom is the prevention of the effectuation of a life entity's priorities. Control is mostly anti-knowledge plus force, and force is anti-effort and this anti-effort prevents the Have-Not from doing something that the Have-Not would otherwise have effectuated.

H. Can we be a little bit more precise in our terms of anti-effort and anti-knowledge?

D. Anti-effort is when one life entity forcefully prevents another life entity from doing something, and anti-knowledge is the prevention of the construction and effectuation of the individual entity's priorities. Both anti-knowledge and anti-effort are

79

inhibitors to freedom. And now, we're able to answer the original question of why it is that control is the main factor by which we can understand the evolution of the political parties.

H. OK, why?

D. It is because of Dictums 1 and 2 that primarily all life does that which is good for it and continually does that which is good for it; and secondly, humans tend to dominate as noted by the principle of Libido Dominandi. It is natural that somebody wants to become a leader, and it is natural that all want to achieve more goodness in everyone's life. As such, one individual necessarily comes to possess more than another individual, and one individual will necessarily devolve to become a leader.

H. And this would make Sir Thomas More's *Utopia* impossible to be implemented into human society.

D. Correct.

H. OK, so now, we have two political parties: the leader who becomes a political party unto himself and those who become subservient to the leader becoming a second political party. But there are various types of leaders, some controlling, some not.

D. Exactly right! It's just a matter of the degree of control that determines the various political parties that can evolve out of a society. It is the degree of control that determines what kind of political party is before us.

H. Well, let's take a look at them one by one and see if this matches up with our definition of the political party according to this one overriding attribute. As for total control, there are the totalitarians. Of course, examples would be North Korea, Cuba,

Venezuela, the former Soviet Union, Pol Pot's Cambodia, and China, to name a few; and in looking these over, these are all considered hard Left ... really extreme Left.

D. Examples of countries with less than totalitarian control are more numerous. We can state all of Western Europe, North America, many in Asia, and much of South America.

H. And, within those countries, there are variations yet as to the amount of control of which the subsequent individual political parties consist, such as here, in the United States between the Democrats and the Republicans. Democrats work toward more control and Republicans less control, although sometimes the line is blurred. But clearly, there is one party that is for less control and that would be the Libertarian Party. So, there are variations in the amount of control that political parties seek to place upon the constituent denizens of our society and others where democratic republics are predominant. So, let me ask you, Professor, why do some parties seek more control over their societal denizens than others? Why the variance? I can see the ultimate variance between the Haves and the Have-Nots, but what about the subtle differences between the Republican and the Democrat here in the United States and the various political parties in Western Europe? Do they all evolve from either the Haves or the Have-Nots? What do you think?

D. Yes, all parties originate from either the Haves or the Have-Nots. The reason why they sometimes come to be blurred and sometimes become indistinguishable from each other is due to the necessity of compromise which is because all these instances are from democratic republics. Since there is a constituency that votes for the individual party members, it's always a battle of ideas, but the ideas all evolve and are generated from the idea of control by either the Haves and, to a lesser extent, the Have-Nots. The doctrine of the Haves is that of control, and the philosophy of the Have-Nots seeks freedom, or at the very least, less control. They both battle over the idea of control. Besides presenting their case to the voting constituency of the nation, they present their cases in the political debate ever unfolding in the media.

H. Ok.

D. As such, the governments of the world tend to move Left for two reasons. First is, as we have discussed before, due to the willingness of both parties to compromise when promoting policies of control due to Dictum 3 which is that the Leftist-Haves feel that the other person is basically bad and the Have-Not-Right feels that the other person is essentially good. Thus, the Right will tend to feel that the other side has some points that are worth looking at and the other side's political proposals may possibly contain some goodness, and as a result, the Right is in general willing to compromise whereas the Left and the totalitarians tend to feel that the other person is bad and the Left is less willing to compromise. Secondly, the offer of free government support by the Haves of the Have-Nots as per the ideology of Noblesse Oblige which is Dictum 4 is also very motivationally powerful. Ergo, the world tends to move Leftward toward greater control as reliance on the Haves to provide governmental support grows and also as governance of societies grows due to Dictum 3. And the will of the Haves to continually assert control will prevail until at some point it reaches a threshold whereby the Have-Nots will vote against the Haves (if the election process is still available) protesting the additional controls placed upon society through Dictums 3 and 4 and revolt against the controls. History has indicated that such a process has transpired repeatedly. However, throughout most of history there was no election process available to the Have-Nots; only the upheaval of the revolt which was always countered with terrible repression by the Haves whenever possible. But there were some Have-Not successful revolutions.

H. What gives the Haves and the Leftist-Haves the energy and ferocity to oppress the Have-Not freedom advocates?

D. It is that the Have-Nots are bad, deplorable, and of no worth except as servants of the Rightly-Guided ones as per Dictum 3; and after the advent of Noblesse Oblige, the Haves have the high moral ground due to Dictum 4.

H. So, now that we've gone over the principles that guide the behavior of the Haves, perhaps we could now apply them to actual circumstances in which history has shown us to be the situation involving the Haves relative to the Have-Nots.

D. Good idea. Let's summarize what we've said before and then explore how these principles can lead us to further observations of the Leftist-Haves. Societies throughout history have always produced a leader. As societies evolve and become larger, the tribe becomes a super-tribe, the leader eventually becomes a king or queen; and as it grows even more, these kings and queens need a group of facilitators and so the Noble class is born, which are their associates to facilitate the effectuation of the edicts, regulations, laws that the king and queen promulgate in their society to allow them to remain the Haves with control over the Have-Nots.

H. OK. Throughout most of history, the Haves have kept the Have-Nots at the bottom without much hope for the future. The Have-Nots are the proletariats, the slaves, and the workers that supply the Haves with products and services along with military might that is needed to protect the Haves or to expand the territory of the Haves to bring further good to the lives of the Haves.

D. As society gathers in its size and becomes more successful evolutionarily speaking, there eventually comes a time when the Haves have need of a cadre of facilitators. In modern-day governmental terms, these facilitators are the government bureaucrats. They are needed to control the Have-Nots and to be able to reap the goods and services that the Have-Nots have produced for the benefit of the Haves which is Dictum 7, that the Haves always seek more control of others and freedom for themselves.

H. Understood.

D. But that's not all that the Haves need when it comes to governance. They also need control of the corporate management in modern societies due to the fact that corporate management controls a significant part of the economy whereby their employees work and pay taxes which we can also call tribute for the facilitators and the government classes right up to the king and queen which are now replaced with the verbiage known as "president," "vice-president," "Congress" and the "government regulators." Thus, the Haves and their associates, the facilitators (also known as government bureaucrats), try on an ongoing basis to forge a relationship with corporate management; and this is commensurate with the various countries of the world that are at least partially fascistic in essence. I suggest, as an example, the oligarchies of Russia and Communist China where there is a crony relationship between the government facilitators and corporate management to the extent that much of the ownership of the companies is controlled by government facilitators, again Dictum 7.

D. Yes! Now there is an interesting statement. You just equated the communist party of China and the present-day oligarchical Russia to be representative fascist governments and that is correct. China is not really truly a communist government in nature. It is actually a fascist country, as is Russia, whereby the government and its facilitators, in essence, own and control the large corporations. Either they own them through possession of stock, or they control the corporations de facto, and as such, the corporations pay the royal and facilitator classes the profits of the corporations through taxation or dividends.

H. Yes, the communist party of China is essentially a totalitarian fascist government. Just as the Soviet Union was, and to some degree, so is present-day Russia.

D. So, throughout modern history, since the Industrial Revolution to the present day, the Haves, along with their facilitators and associates, try to forge agreements with the entities that generate successful production of goods and services of society. They do this by control, the nature of which we have just discussed.

H. Yes, the Haves initiate control eliminating the potential for cooperation because they believe that the nature of the serfs, proletariats, and the slaves in the lower class is inherently bad as per Dictum 3. They believe so because of various examples, such as, the Have-Nots are bad because they are just not of the social stature of the Haves, or the Have-Nots are just not of the intellectual quality of the Haves.

D. Another reason that the Have-Nots are looked down upon by the Haves is because of Dictum 5, that power tends to corrupt and absolute power corrupts absolutely.

H. Right. We have shown that this is true because when you

become all-controlling, you no longer have to cooperate, and instead you can use your own priorities without referring to the priorities of others. When you only refer to your own priorities, you become bumptious and full of yourself allowing for your point of view to become the only perspective, which becomes one's reality and becomes the only one that one perceives without adding in the knowledge and sentiments of others. Thus, the knowledge to make important decisions at the top becomes inefficient and unreasonable because of their non-inclusion of the knowledge produced by others in society.

D. And this will provide us with an amazing conclusion. The progress in the evolution of the societies that are controlled by the few will tend to get worse without exception.

H. I'm sorry I do not understand what you're talking about.

D. In all societies that are controlled by the Haves, that is to say, in all societies that are controlled by the few without input by others such as allowed by democratic societies, the progress of these hyper-controlling societies will necessarily and 100% be relatively little compared to the open societies that democratic republics produce.

H. And the reason for this again? Is it all because of Dictum 5, the Lord Acton Principle?

D. Yes. The reason is due to the production of knowledge within a society. Societies with a greater amount of freedom and less control produce more knowledge. As you know from our previous conversations, knowledge is the predominant factor in the philosophic economic equation of the Sacrifice equals the Reward. As societies advance, this predominant, salient factor of knowledge becomes even more prevalent and more necessary and takes up a greater percentage of the sacrifice versus the reward equation. Knowledge is the major component of all products and services. As society evolves, the percentage of knowledge that makes up the Sacrifice/Reward equation increases to become the major factor in the production of all goods and services and is the major factor in the advancement of society and the amount of goodness that society produces. The more society is controlled by the Haves, the more society necessarily degrades, and its ability to produce better goods and services becomes less and less because the production of knowledge becomes limited due to the Lord Acton Principle which we also call Dictum 5.

Chapter 4 - Summary

————————•o◇o•————————

H. So, Professor, I think at this point, let's list up the principles of the Haves and the Have-Nots.

D. There are seven political behavior principles of the Rightly-Guided Haves:

Dictum 1: The Law of Demand for the Good
Dictum 2: St. Augustine's Principle of Libido Dominandi (The will to Dominate, Control, and Compete with others)
Dictum 3: The Have-Nots are inherently not good (The Rationale of Control)
Dictum 4: Noblesse Oblige (Control through Contract)
Dictum 5: The Lord Action Principle that power corrupts and absolute power corrupts absolutely (Nature of Control)
Dictum 6: The end justifies the means (The Unethical Rationale of Control)
Dictum 7: The Haves always seek more control of others and freedom for themselves. (The Essence of the Leftist-Haves)

There are seven political behavior principles of the Have-Nots:

Dictum 1: The Law of Demand for the Good
Dictum 2: St. Augustine's Principle of Libido Dominandi (The Will to Dominate, Control, and Compete with others)
Dictum 3: Both the Haves & the Have-Nots are inherently good (The Rationale to Cooperate)
Dictum 4: There is a duty to sustain freedom. (The Rationale That There is a Right to Freedom)
Dictum 5: Absolute freedom begets ethicalities absolutely (The

Rationale that Freedom to Cooperate to Produce Desiderata will Result in an Ethical & Charitable Society)

Dictum 6: Ethics = The appropriate dispensation of respect (The Nature of Ethics)

Dictum 7: The Haves-Nots seek liberty for all. (The Essence of the Conservative Right)

H. These are the principles that distinguish political thought?

D. Yes.

H. So, I think that at this point we should speak about the Have-Nots. As I see from the list of Dictums that they have some variations that are not commensurate with the political behavior principles of the Haves. The first two Dictums are the same. However, the third Dictum is the opposite as we noted previously.

D. Right. The Haves believe that the Have-Nots are inherently not good people in their essence and the Have-Nots believe that all people are inherently good, or at least, have some good within them. As we have spoken before, this is the rationale that allows the Have-Nots to be more cooperative than the Haves. As such, governments throughout the world tend to move toward the philosophy of the Haves and generally become more controlling of the Have-Nots.

H. Yes.

D. And these facilitators control the Have-Nots through motivation and through negative knowledge plus force; and of course, examples of the negative knowledge are the rules, regulations, and laws coming from the government into the hands of the facilitators who use them to control the Have-Nots.

H. Yes, negative knowledge is that which obstructs the production of our desiderata which includes the production of goods and services through the use of edicts, proclamations, laws, and regulations that prevent us from being more efficient. Of course, I understand we need some laws and regulations because it helps to promote society such as through the creation of our judicial system. But in that case, these laws and regulations are actually positive knowledge because it promotes cooperation within society and settles arguments to prevent a breakdown within society.

D. Now, because of Dictum 4 of Noblesse Oblige, the Haves will think that they should provide this social net for the Have-Nots. They have motivation to do so, and it is twofold: first, they think that they should give welfare funds to the Have-Nots in exchange for their votes and loyalty; and they think they should give welfare in order to assuage the lower classes so that they feel that they have an adequate social net to provide for their living and will not rise up in a revolution with violent harmful consequences directed toward the Haves. And this is common among societies of the communists, fascists, and socialists. The kings, queens, and the royalty of the past did not have this sense of Noblesse Oblige because in times of yore, there was no motivation to do so. However, the French revolutions (of 1789 and 1848 along with writers of socialism and communism, e.g. Marx and Engels) helped to change that, and the motivation to supply the Have-Nots with a minimum living standard appeared. Once this methodology or political philosophy appeared, then the ideologies of the communism, socialism, and fascism came to be along with their cadres of secret police and other forms of oppression control that prevents the proletariat slaves from rising up against the Haves also known as the ruling class.

H. So, the ideology of Noblesse Oblige is really for the

continuation of the control of the Have-Nots. So, looking back over history, the control of the Have-Nots was worse and more oppressive until they fought back.

D. Yes, and the oppression was exacerbated because of Dictum 5 which is the Lord Acton Principle which abolished the need and propensity for cooperation.

H. But there are some in the lower classes who do not submit to the control and do not want to continue in serfdom, slavery, and be a worker bee for their entire life and work for the Haves. There are those Have-Nots that want to break out of the serfdom class.

D. They want to break out and go to the middle class because of Dictum 1 that all life wants that which is good for it and continually wants that which is good for it.

H. Yes, I understand because now it can be thought and considered by the Haves that these non-cooperative serfs or proletariats that adhere to Dictum 1 are basically bad people. The Haves and their facilitators will consider them inherently bad due to Dictum 3.

D. And therefore, there is no respect for the individual rights of these Have-Nots whether they are conformists (staying in their subservient class) or non-conformists (jumping up into the middle class). In the eyes of the Haves, they are inherently bad people that need to be controlled; and negative knowledge plus force is used to control the Have-Nots.

H. Yes, we have established that negative knowledge plus force equals control.

D. And this control is absolutely needed by the Haves. They need this control in order to distribute economic profits equally and allow equity in the social justice of the Have-Nots whereby everybody stays where they are in society and whereby everybody is equal in every way. It is as if they are seeking the same as what Sir Thomas More described in his book, *Utopia*.

H. Which is impossible because as we discussed in *Utopia*, there is no consideration of the fact that all human life needs motivation in order to make decisions. People don't do things without motivation. Societal denizens are not going to constantly help others without recompense or compensation for one's sacrifice as it would violate Dictum 1.

D. Further, the Rightly-Guided Leftist Haves believe that the Have-Nots have a bad nature as we know from Dictum 3; and because they are bad, there is no empathy for the Have-Not advocate of individual rights. Therefore, the lower classes are downtrodden, and as such, the Haves enforce the lower class to be equal in every way such as in opportunity, standard of living, or way of life; and they do so because their only purpose is to serve the Haves; thus, from the Haves' point of view, it is best they stay in their lower class.

H. Pure communism! And to be known as a "deplorable"! What a miserable awful existence!

D. This is what I would call caste-fascism.

H. Well, I would agree. But let me ask you a question. Why would the non-conformist of the lower class, of the lower slave, serf, proletariat, and workingman class, be bad if they were to jump out and create a middle class? Why would these "irredeemables" which pay taxes, are bad, and known as the "deplorables" be allowed to jump out of the lower class to create a middle class?

D. They are not only deplorable but they are non-conformist by jumping out of the lower caste class: it is inexcusable; they are not allowed!

H. But why?

D. Jumping out of the surf class causes a problem for the facilitators. And sometimes it can cause a really bad problem if there's a violent breakout as per the examples of the French revolutions and other revolutions also. But the first and basic violation of jumping out of the surf class is the violation of Dictum 4, Noblesse Oblige.

H. I see. When the serf jumps out of the lower class, he's violating the contract of Noblesse Oblige. The Rightly-Guided Leftist Haves provide a guaranteed minimum wage which is a welfare of sorts for which the serf receives a guarantee from the Haves in exchange for an oath of loyalty. It's a contract. The Haves will give largesse for their fealty to the system by the Have-Nots.

D. Exactly! When a Have-Not jumps out of his class into the middle class, he violates the contract, and therefore, they are viewed by the Haves as a non-conformist, as unethical, and as deplorable. The Leftist Haves believe that the Have-Nots do this for two reasons: because the Have-Nots are inherently bad people as per Dictum 3; and the Have-Nots are unethical since they have broken the Noblesse Oblige contract. As a result, the Haves believe that there is no reason for the Haves to cooperate with the non-conformist Have-Nots anymore.

H. Ok

D. And if there is no need to cooperate with them, then it means that the Haves may employ the end justifies the means rationality in dealing with the deplorables, the serfs, and the non-conformist Have-Nots, as per Dictum 6.

H. Oh right! This gives the rationale by the Leftist-Haves to freely lie, and do other unethical behavior or actions against the Have-Not-Right with mental and psychological impunity! This explains a lot: the Haves could, and have, and do, deftly lie and use unethical behavior toward the Have-Not-Right when the Haves-Nots have behaved not in accordance to the original Noblesse Oblige social contract whereby the Have-Nots try to jump out of their original proletariat class. This is an outstanding and amazing generalization, but it seems to be a valid conclusion from what we've established so far. I wondered if it could be shown to be true, factually, and statistically.

D. Well, we have our everyday experience in watching the media to give us our impressions as to whether this is true or not.

H. It certainly seems that way.

D. But to get back to a point about the Have-Nots jumping out of their lower class, there's a second problem that develops for the Haves. This is that the jumping out by the Have-Nots causes a morality problem. This is because the non-conformity of the jump-out causes an inequity in the serf class. The inequality is that somebody is acquiring and achieving more goodness for himself than the rest of the serf class. Therefore, this is an unethical action by these Have-Nots that they have now gone to the middle class. They leave their brothers and sisters behind and will, and do acquire more goodness than those in the serf, proletariat class. First, it is deplorably selfish of these Have-Nots, and this is morally wrong in the eyes of the Haves as they are the caretakers of the Have-Nots. Hence, for the sake of the remaining Have-Nots in the lower class, they rail, criticize, and object to the fugitive Have-Nots that have escaped.

H. Makes sense. I have seen them in the news use all sorts of pejoratives directed toward these Have-Nots that have escaped such as "racist" and "supremacist" to name just a couple.

D. The worst sin that can be made by the Have-Nots is to jump out to the middle class, become prosperous, then arrogate unto themselves the airs and powers of the Facilitator/Noble/King Class while remaining and representing the Have-Not Class. This is a mortal sin, and when it occurs, it must be stamped out and the Have-Not must be put back into the proletariat class and done so at any cost without regard to any considerations of morality.

H. As the end justifies the means philosophy prevails for the Leftist-Haves, I can surely think of a couple of obvious examples in the current political arena to which this by-any-means-possible-mentality applies.

D. But there's a problem with this type of thinking for the Leftist-Have. The problem is as we had mentioned, the First Dictum of Life. Life doesn't want to be controlled because it seeks that which is good for it and continually seeks that which is good for it. Life wants to pursue goodness for itself, its offspring, and to a lesser degree society, for those with whom the individuals cooperate.

H. Right. We already pointed out that life seeks goodness by making sacrifices to receive a reward; after all, the sacrifice equals the reward is an equation that we've gone over in a previous conversation that I put to print.

D. And this equation produces betterment and improvement by increasing its components.

H. To review, these components are risk, information, knowledge, time, and energy (or force); and if it's a product as opposed to a service, we should add in material to the constituent variables. As we have noted before, we can actually make an equation that could represent the basic economic transaction as follows:

$$S_{(R,I,T,E(M))} = R_{(R,I,T,E(M))}$$

D. Right. Within the constituent variables, most of the improvements come through the information-knowledge variable which improves the sacrifice and thereby improves the reward. Therefore, as knowledge improves, so does life and the differentiation of the creativity of the new products and services that it produces. And the Haves tend to suppress the accumulation of knowledge by the production of anti-knowledge.

H. Yes, as already mentioned.

D. The Left must also suppress per force this accumulation of knowledge by the Have-Nots. They must because as knowledge accumulates, the Have-Nots become Haves incrementally. As such, these Have-Nots would begin to become part of a Nouveau Riche Class.

H. And I suppose the Haves will be by and large against that.

D. The Have-Nots will tend to become politically conservative because, in the production of the resultant Rewards from the Sacrifices, cooperation is needed in order to become successful. As a consequence, cooperation increases whilst the Have-Nots believe and trust in the goodness of others.

H. Ok.

D. And cooperation equals knowledge of an efficiency of the newly combined sacrifice with others as the constituent individuals who are cooperating understand that it is more efficient to combine together and cooperate to produce a good or service than it is, separately or individually, to try to effectuate the production of the service or product.

H. Yes, and we know from *The Nature of Ethics: Defining Ethics Good & Evil* that cooperation is possible by the effusion of respect; and the appropriate dispensation of respect is the essence of ethics. We respect others in order to cooperate, and we cooperate in order to produce goods and services which bring us up away from misery which is the nature of that which is the good. Therefore, we can conclude that this increasing amount of cooperation produces greater goodness in the conservative base.

D. Yes, that's essentially true because this reasoning can explain why the South switched over to being Republican whereas many years ago, or many decades ago, it was predominantly Democratic. It did so because its economy gradually transformed itself to a knowledge-based economy from an agrarian one. But there's another conclusion that we can make. This conclusion is that the Democratic Party does not grow naturally when knowledge is increasing in a society.

H. What!?

D. Therefore, the socialist Haves search for new sources of voters with lesser degrees of accumulated knowledge which will allow them to continue to a system of creating caste-socialism and keeping their base constituent voters under control to work for the Haves in both totalitarian and democratic republic societies. In any Have-controlled society, the Have-Nots will need to work for the Haves, pay taxes (also known as tribute) to the Haves, receive welfare (or a job) from the Haves, and receive the basic necessities of life from the Haves fulfilling Dictum 4.

H. Wow!

D. And thus, the Haves will naturally control the unions because the unions are made up of the workers that are all approximately the same in the degree of knowledge under which they operate; that is, they are uniform in the amount of knowledge they possess in order to do their jobs. Differentiation of human services is of no concern to the unions.

H. Very interesting.

D. And so in the union situation, they will work to make everybody equal in knowledge and suppress the Law of Differentiation which causes new products and services to be produced.

H. Right! Otherwise, they would leave the plantation!

D. As a democratic society prospers through the increase in knowledge (assuming elections are fair), the Haves will lose voters and will actually become a minority party.

H. Well, it makes sense. The Haves - also now known as the Democratic Party - lose voters because its voters are becoming prosperous going from the Have-Nots to the Nouveau Riche segment of society by increasing their knowledge and not needing Dictum 4 and the Democratic Party anymore!

D. The Haves, given the chance, will always try to get ahold of the election process; and when they would get full control of the government, they would never give it up. Elections would become unfair and controlled!

H. How do we know this?

D. We know this emphatically from history. Whenever the Left gets a hold of a nation, they get hold of the ballot box also. Looking back in history, all we have to do is remember Nazi Germany. Look at Pol Pot, look at Mao, look at Stalin, look at Fascist Italy under Mussolini, and the list goes on. Most recently look at Venezuela! And look at the Communist Party of China and North Korea! They all got control of the ballot box and the election mechanisms (if there were any to begin with).

H. That's right! But maybe one could say that the Right, or that is, the Have-Nots, would do the same thing in controlling the ballot box.

D. But it does not! Prima facie, if it did, the founding of this country with its Constitution and Bill of Rights would have been impossible. But it was possible because the Have-Nots believe that people are basically good; and because they are basically good, they should be treated equally before the law.

H. But for the Haves, is this problem of the first Dictum the entire problem that stands in their way of total control of the Have-Nots? I would not think in old times when the Haves, or that is, the royalty, which would consist of a king and queen and its nobility, that this first Dictum would have mattered much. The royalty and the upper class would have ruled the roost, as it were, and an opportunity to jump up to the middle class would have been limited and difficult, to say the least, right up until the advent of the revolutions, so there must be another problem that presents itself to the Haves in order to maintain its control of society.

D. Yes, it is the problem when the Haves are within a representative democracy whereby the Haves must compete for the votes of the societal constituents.

H. Yes, I see. They must go into a propaganda mode bloviating about the need for a social net, income inequality, opportunity inequality, racial inequality, racial supremacy of one group over another, the importance of uniform equity, or discrimination of one sort or another because if they do not, only their thirty percent base would vote for them as everybody else in voting society would be too busy trying to fulfill Dictum 1.

D. And if the subject of the propaganda were not revolving around the examples you just mentioned, the Haves would concentrate on a different set because the human species is replete with faults as nobody is perfect in any way except for Jesus. As Saint Paul said, all have sinned, and come short of the glory of God. There is no shortage of subject matter if we are looking to point out the depravity of mankind. We all have sins and failures, even the Haves. After all, Dictum 3 of the Haves will be fulfilled.

H. The Haves have no shortage of subject matter to rail against when speaking of society all the while speaking of themselves as saviors of society in order to get votes.

D. This explains why the Haves are not friends with the churchgoers as the Lord Jesus Christ comes into direct conflict with them as the saviors of society. So, in order to vanquish this source of competition, the Haves would try to appropriate the power of any religion that is propinquant to the Have-Nots of the society.

100

H. Wow! This is exactly the history of the church and state throughout history. My gosh, look at the history of the Catholic Church, with its symbiotic relationship with the Haves, selling its product, penance, to the royalty and upper class (the Haves) amassing huge wealth while the Haves receive permission from the Church to execute its edicts, laws, and regs with the Church's blessing so that both stay in power fulfilling Have-Dictums 1, 2, 4, 6, and 7.

D. Of course, this is not limited to the Catholic Church; look at the societies of Islam, whose relationship between the clerics and the state are even closer. In Islam, the church - or should I say the mosque - and the state are one and the same, completely fulfilling all Dicta of the Haves. In Islam, the clerics have direct access to the political powers in all its societies with only minimal and few exceptions. Historically, all factions of the Islamic royalty class had to vie for the control of society in whatever capacity and through a coalition necessary to accomplish the consummation of being the ultimate Have which in their terms would be the Caliph.

H. Did you say "had to vie"?

D. Like everybody, the Haves also are subject to Dictum 2.

H. We have delineated the principles of the Haves and the Have-Nots and the first two are the same for both. However, in the third Dictum, differences arise and diverge in that the Haves view others as not having a good nature, and the Have-Nots view others as being of a good nature. This brings us to Dictum 4, Noblesse Oblige, where the Haves view themselves as the praetorian guard of the less fortunate of society, the providers of societal morality and a requisite social net, while the Have-Nots view that there is not a requisite obligation by the royalty and facilitator classes to be responsible for the less fortunate of society, but it is the province of the denizens of the resident country to volunteer charity; and we have already concluded that it would probably be most efficient for society to help the less fortunate through a combination of government assisting private charity to execute the social net. I think we can safely say that the government class should participate by disseminating its tax revenue to the nonprofit organizations and let the nonprofits effectuate the administration and dissemination of the welfare funds instead of the government which, as everybody agrees, is very inefficient, to say the least.

D. Yes. An understatement to be sure.

H. This brings us to Dictum 5, the Lord Acton Principle, which is applicable to the Haves, but it appears from our list that the Have-Nots are not subject to it. It says that absolute freedom begets ethicalities absolutely. May I ask how is this?

D. Let's work it through. While recalling that freedom is the creation of one's priorities and the effectuation of these priorities, we know that chief among our priorities is our desideratum to do that which is good for us; further, we know that ethics is the appropriate dispensation of respect, and respect is the evolutionary behavioral mechanism that allows humans to cooperate; and we cooperate because it allows us to be more efficient in producing our goods and services which brings us up away from misery which is the essence of that which is good. Therefore, freedom allows us to effectuate our goodness through the use of ethical behavior which allows us to cooperate to produce efficiently that which is good for us. Thus, we may conclude that freedom propels us to be ethical. Control, the opposite of cooperation, takes us down the road of non-ethical, or a-ethical, behavior through the unethical ideology of the end justifies the means which eschews cooperation substituting in its stead the use of control.

H. Again, wow! An indictment of those Rightly-Guided Haves that seek control! It appears that we may conclude that politicians who work to garner control of society are tendentiously unethical.

D. Freedom is the basis by which man strives to produce goods and services through ethical behavior which generates products that contain goodness as that which is good brings this up away from misery which is the essence of that which is good.

H. Ergo, freedom pro-generates goodness, and therefore, the opposite of that - control - brings us toward misery.

D. Control is anti-freedom and brings forth anti-knowledge, and thus, an inefficiency in producing goods and services which bring us up away from misery and thus reduces the amount of goodness within society through decreasing the amount of knowledge available to society and decreasing the amount of knowledge being generated in an ongoing basis in society.

H. An amazing, cogent conclusion. It indicates why totalitarian societies do not provide the advancement in the production of goodness for mankind. It gives us an understanding of why North Korea, the Communist Party of China (which is really in essence should be nominated as the Fascist Society of China), Cuba, the nations of Islam, and all totalitarian societies of yore, will, over time, fall behind societies that protect its freedoms for the Have-Nots. All the totalitarian Leftist regimes throughout history even to the present without exception have visited misery upon whom they control.

D. There is another amazing conclusion which is that the free market economy, also known as capitalism, is the only ethical system of society and the most efficacious way to produce goodness for society in the most efficient manner.

H. Yes, I can see that this is a conclusion that we could draw from our principle that absolute freedom begets ethicalities absolutely! It appears this is the exact opposite of the Lord Acton Principle. We could introduce it as the corollary to the Lord Acton Principle.

D. Sounds good!

H. Well, this opens us up to the obvious next question: what is free-market capitalism? From what we have just discussed, it is not as it is defined in economic textbooks.

D. That is right. The textbooks are not incorrect; it is that they just don't inform us of its nature and essence. Let's get together again tomorrow to continue this discussion.

H. OK. Thanks for giving me this time today, and I will drop by tomorrow morning.

D. Haskell, good day to you.

H. And to you, Professor.

Chapter 5 – The Philosophical Definition
of Free Market Enterprise

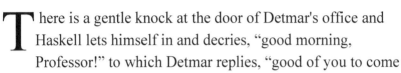

T here is a gentle knock at the door of Detmar's office and
Haskell lets himself in and decries, "good morning,
Professor!" to which Detmar replies, "good of you to come
back to discuss the nature of capitalism which may lead us to
further revelations!"

H. Excellent! It sounds like it will be an exciting day! I am
loaded with interrogatories.

D. I am glad to assist with the new book.

H. Thank you! To begin with, I went home after yesterday's
interview and in anticipation of today's subject matter, I opened up
a book or two and noted some examples of definitions of the free
market. I noticed that they are all unremarkable and tautological
leading us to no inspiration as to the nature and essence of free-
market capitalism.

D. For instance?

H. From one of the dictionaries, it said that the free market is an
economy operating by free competition, and the second definition
from that dictionary was an economic market or system in which
prices are based on competition among private businesses and not
controlled by a government.

D. Sounds OK.

H. From another source, it said that the free market is based on supply and demand without government control and consists of voluntary exchanges and is characterized by decentralized economic decisions based on legal rules.

D. That's a little better.

H. And from the Library of Economics & Freedom, Murray Rothbard says that the free market is "a summary term for an array of exchanges that take place in society. Each exchange is undertaken as a voluntary agreement between two people or between groups of people represented by agents. These two individuals (or agents) exchange two economic goods, either tangible commodities or non-tangible services."

D. I am an admirer of Murray Rothbard.

H. Lastly, from another source, it says that the free market is where buyers and sellers can make their deals through supply and demand, and the stock market is a good example of this.

D. The stock market does come close to this ideal.

H. Well, I noticed that all of these definitions have the same problem which is to say that none of them define "free," or "market," or any of the other terms that they come up with such as "competition" or "exchange." So, in other words, economic textbooks really do not enlighten us as to the nature of free-market capitalism, or should I say free-market enterprise.

D. That's right!

H. So, where do we start, Professor?

D. The philosophical definition of the essence of the free market is composed of one dictum plus six corollaries.

H. What? Pray tell, good sir!

D. Well naturally, the initial dictum of economics is the same as the first Dictum of political thought: life seeks that which is good for it, and it is a never-ending search for that which is good for it.

H. Why am I not surprised?

D. And you will not be surprised then at Corollary 1 which is the nature of freedom.

H. Freedom is the construction of priorities and then the effectuation of those priorities.

D. And the effectuation of a priority is our sacrifice that we make in order to receive a reward.

H. It is just as we discussed yesterday and as we have previously discussed in *The Philosophical Equations of Economics*.

D. Corollary 2 is, as we have discussed previously, the equation that the Sacrifice equals the Reward.

H. We sacrifice our time, effort, and material, and we use our information and knowledge within an atmosphere of risk to achieve a reward. And we can make the equation as previously noted. If it's a service instead of a physical product, then we just take out material from the equation.

D. Once freedom is established; that is, once the priorities are established and allowed to be effectuated, then motivation appears. And so, motivation is Corollary 3 which is the comparative relationship between the sacrifice and the reward; and we can make a little equation to represent it where "M" is motivation: $M = (S{:}R)$. And so the sacrifice relative to the reward is the amount of motivation present in any decision that we may encounter in our lives. With every decision in our lives, we come face-to-face with the amount of sacrifice that it requires and the amount of reward that we would receive comparative and relative to the sacrifice, and this ratio is our motivation.

H. Understood.

D. And one way to receive a reward efficiently is to sometimes join up with others in a cooperative manner to achieve the reward. Manufacturing is almost entirely a cooperative venture of people working together sacrificing their time, and effort, and using their knowledge to achieve a reward.

H. Yes, we've been through this.

D. Cooperative behavior is the sacrifice of two or more persons to obtain a reward; and they sacrifice their collective knowledge, time, and effort, amidst an environment of risk to obtain a reward. Both of these people (or more, together cumulatively) will be sacrificing their time, effort, and knowledge (and sometimes their material) in an atmosphere of risk to produce either goods or services.

H. Right.

D. And we make the sacrifices together to get the common reward because the participants perceive that the reward has goodness, thus, fulfilling Dictum 1 and Corollary 1 whereby the sacrifice equals the reward.

H. Yes.

D. Corollary 4 is cooperation; that is, cooperative behavior is the sacrifice that individuals make in order to achieve a reward for each participant, and each participant has the additional knowledge that each participant will have a greater efficiency together than if alone.

H. Yes, when individual members of a society band together as a cooperative to produce something, that is, a good or service, they do so in realizing that the cooperative group becomes more efficient than if the individual participants were to struggle to make the same product individually, alone.

D. In essence, when the participants realize that as a group they can produce more goodness than they could individually and that this extra goodness accrues to the individuals themselves, the individuals decide to cooperate together because there is an incentive to do so which is the extra goodness. Incentive fulfills Corollary 3 and goodness fulfills Dictum 1.

H. Ok.

D. And in order to produce cooperative behavior which is the effort of our sacrifice and the knowledge that working together with other people will result in the greater ability to produce goods and services which is good and which will allow us to live better, we will consider others, with whom we cooperate, important to our lives; and thus, we will make instruments of cooperation, such as agreements, covenants, contracts.

H. Yes, there are many types of agreements such as individuals with individuals; companies with companies; society with government; and I suppose a good example of an agreement between society and government would be the creation of property rights.

D. And it is important to know that within any contract or agreement, there are rights and obligations. There is a right to receive something and there is an obligation to give something for each party involved. For example, if you're in a store and you go to the cash-out register, your obligation is to give the payment for the object that you want to buy to the cashier; and it is your right to receive that object. Again, across from you is the cashier, whose obligation is to give you the object that you wish to purchase and their right is to receive your money.

H. Well, as we discussed regarding the essence of a privilege, a contract or agreement equals the possession of an obligation and a right for each participant. And, therefore, a right may only exist inside an agreement or contract.

D. However, there is a byproduct of the societal freedom of Corollary 1, and that is the convergence of priorities. That is, others in society may come to have the same priorities as another as all life seeks that which is good for it, and this would cause the appearance of competition where multiple life entities seek the same goodness. Ergo, competition emerges as per the convergence of priorities. To wit, it naturally emerges from two factors: 1) from the existence of freedom; and 2) from Saint Augustine's principle of Libido Dominandi (Dictum 2, the lust for dominion; the desire to dominate) which is also Corollary 5 of the free market economy.

H. Oh yes, I can see the reason why we have to include this principle in the nature of the free market. It is because competition is the convergence of priorities and converging priorities are inimical to the health of the life entity. All companies, individuals, and societies know that direct competition can take away from available resources. In the economic arena, it makes it harder to get customers. But yet, competition exists. It exists because, within human nature, there is this will to compete which evolved in the human species. This will to compete becomes genetically inherent within life entities and has evolved within the human species also; and Saint Augustine noted this proclivity of the human species and deemed it to be the principle of Libido Dominandi, also known here as Dictum 2.

D. And thus, coming from Dictum 2 of the political philosophical principles and Corollary 5 from the definition of free market enterprise is born the will to compete. Competition equals the convergence of the priorities by two or more entities which is a by-product of Corollary 1 plus Dictum 2.

H. Ok.

D. This brings us to Corollary 6 which is the Law of Differentiation that you wrote about in *The Philosophical Equations of Economics*.

H. The Law of Differentiation says that there is divergence from the market priorities fulfilling new demand to deliver new goodness as all life knows that direct competition is inimical to one's health; so it attempts to diverge away through differentiation. This law produces the variations of products in the marketplace.

D. And this Law of Differentiation is consistent with political philosophy in that freedom is required for its existence, and hence, it sits inside Dictum 1 which is the Law of the Demand for the Good.

H. Interesting!

D. And so to summarize, we can actually make an equation for the definition of free market enterprise using as its basis the economic transaction which you delineated in *The Philosophical Equations of Economics* which is that the Sacrifice equals the Reward.

Free market enterprise equals:

The Good (Dictum 1) + Freedom (Corollary 1) + Sacrifice = Reward (Corollary 2) + Motivation (S:R which is Corollary 3) + Cooperation (Corollary 4) + Competition (Corollary 5) + the Law of Differentiation (Corollary 6).

H. Why is Dictum 1, a Dictum and all the rest Corollaries?

D. Dictum 1 is the central principle because all the Corollaries fit inside of it and in some of the other Have-Not Dictums as well. We can see this if we parse the equation.

H. The good is that all life does that which is good for it and continually does that which is good for it. Freedom is the creation of priorities and the effectuation of these priorities to achieve goodness and inhabits Dictums 1, 4, 5, 6, & 7. The sacrifice is the consummation of our information knowledge, time, effort, and sometimes the material in an environment of risk to achieve a reward in which there is perceived goodness (Dictum 1). Motivation is the ratio of the amount of sacrifice relative to the reward (Dictum 1); cooperation is the knowledge that we can be more efficient in concert with others than if alone (Dictums 1 & 3). Competition is the convergence of priorities plus Libido Dominandi (Dictum 2). The Law of Differentiation says that all of life will try to differentiate to avoid direct competition whether it be short-term economic differentiation conducted by companies diversifying their product line to make their products stand out and be noticed for the consumer goodness inherent within the good or service or the evolution of species which seek differentiation into an ecological niche. And all life entities are subject to the Law of Differentiation (Dictum 1 & 2).

D. Very good. So, as we take a look at these Corollaries, we can see that there is an opportunity to generate an equation that will describe the various elements that you just listed.

H. That equation would be the general economic equation of the sacrifice equals the reward that we came up with in *The Philosophical Equations of Economics*.

D. And that is representative of Dictum 1, and the Corollaries are representative of the various variables that inhabit the general equation. The base equation is as we just noted:

The Good (Dictum 1) + Freedom (Corollary 1) + Sacrifice = Reward (Corollary 2) + Motivation (S:R which is Corollary 3) + Cooperation (Corollary 4) + Competition (Corollary 5) + the Law of Differentiation (Corollary 6)

Which we could denote as:

$$dt\|v_{(Convergent\text{-}Divergent)}\|Sacrifice = (R_{(\%)}(K_{(byte\text{-}ergs)} +$$
$$C_{(Cooperate\ Knowledge\ of\ Efficiency)})^{T}(sec)^{E}(ergs)^{M}(mass)) :$$
$$Rwd_{(The\ Good)} = (R_{(\%)}{}^{K}{}_{(byte\text{-}ergs)}{}^{T}(sec)^{E}(ergs)^{M}(mass))$$

$$+$$

Other Transactional Equations from others who are willing to cooperate to produce a Good or Service

Freedom is represented by the creation and effectuation of knowledge and this is noted by a knowledge base; motivation is the comparison of the two sides of the equation; cooperation is the combining of the equations when multiple individuals are striving together by the C variable; competition and differentiation would be the change in the product of the sacrifice and reward sides of the equation over a period of time as the product of the equation either converges or diverges represented by vector analysis and noted as $\|v\|$.

H. Yes, I see your point in this pro forma equation noting the possible inclusion of calculus and vector analysis to describe the entire situation of Free Market Enterprise. I see now that we could put this concept entirely into one equation. Further, the product of the sacrifice and reward sides could be put into a Cartesian graph which would have as its dimensions the quantity of each variable at any time and then the differentiation of the resultant vector could be calculated to note, in a field of competitors, the niche location of the company or life entity's action. As this location converges or diverges away from each other, competition or differentiation could be tracked.

D. Right.

H. We could say that the sacrifice equaling the reward to be the function of the spatial coordinates $x, y, z,$ equals risk, knowledge + cooperative knowledge, and time equals the resultant vector. And then, we could describe competition and differentiation as the difference of the resultant vector noted as $\|v\|$ over time.

D. Yes.

H. So, on to my next two questions. We have noted that the sacrifice equals the reward; but how does that come to be? How is it possible? I mean to say that first, we use our freedom to decide to effectuate our priority by embarking on our sacrifice which ultimately becomes a reward; but they are different. As an example, let's assume we are hunter-gatherers and we hunt with spears. Then one individual invents the bow and arrow, and it is more efficient than a spear. So, suddenly a physical bow and arrow lessen the risk of hunting, the time it takes, the effort involved, and changes the knowledge of how to hunt and the material of the bow and arrow which is the sacrifice side of the equation that transmutes the reward side of the equation into animal meat that was the object of these ingredients. How does the sacrifice equal the reward as the bow and arrow do not equal an animal's carcass and its resultant meat and nutrition? What happens that allows the sacrifice to become the reward?

D. It is not a transmutation. It is an exchange whereby the sacrifice of the hunter which involves his risk of being outside hunting, the effort which includes the force of the kill involved in the hunt, the time it requires, the materials being used such as the bow and arrow, and the knowledge and information involved in the process of the hunt is exchanged for the prize of nutrition (albeit, an involuntary exchange on the animal's part as there is no agreement in place that predicates the exchange which would be present in voluntary exchanges that are processed in a societal market).

H. OK, but we must also consider if a transmutation is present in a more complicated event such as an exchange of someone giving his money in an exchange for a product at a retail vendor of some sort.

D. Still, it is not a transmutation; it is an exchange of two products or services of perceived like or similar value due to the priorities, which are the basis of knowledge, that indicate the degree to which the goods and or services are important to us. Each side of the transaction has a sacrifice and a reward, and in a cooperative society that generates these goods and services, the concept of transmutation is replaced by the manufacturing of that which is good for us; and then if desired, one would trade it for something else that is further desired.

H. Yes, I recall now. The transaction of the sacrifice equaling the reward is present for each participant. A person will make a sacrifice to achieve a reward, and once the reward is received, he may swap it for the reward of another who has produced it from that person's sacrifice. And so now, I understand that it is an exchange of perceived value, not a transmutation.

D. Correct.

Chapter 6: The Nature of Peace

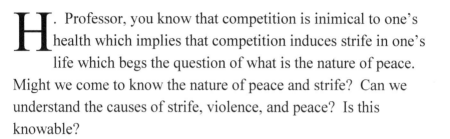

H. Professor, you know that competition is inimical to one's health which implies that competition induces strife in one's life which begs the question of what is the nature of peace. Might we come to know the nature of peace and strife? Can we understand the causes of strife, violence, and peace? Is this knowable?

D. Yes.

H. Great! Let's start with the nature of peace.

D. Peace is the fulfillment of life's first Dictum: life seeks that which is good for it and it continually seeks that which is good for it. When we freely seek that which is good for us, we are at peace.

H. What? That's it?

D. First, in order to continually seek that which is good for us, we need freedom. As we recall, freedom is the construction of priorities and then the effectuation of those priorities.

H. And the effectuation of a priority is a sacrifice that we make in order to receive a reward, and we have established that our sacrifices equal our rewards. We sacrifice our time, effort, and material, and we use our information and knowledge within an atmosphere of risk to achieve our rewards. As I have written, we can make an equation of this general situation which would be: The Sacrifice = The Reward.

D. Then once freedom is established, that is, once the priorities

117

are established, then peace requires motivation (Corollary 3), and it is the comparative relationship between the sacrifice and the reward. Thus,

$$M = (S:R)$$

H. OK, however, I suspect that this situation is when one is at peace with oneself and does not really extend or explain societal peace. I think you are speaking about individual peace.

D. That is correct. As you know, in order to receive many rewards efficiently, one would join up with others in society in a cooperative manner to achieve one or more rewards. Manufacturing is almost entirely a cooperative venture of people sacrificing their time, effort, materials, and using their knowledge to achieve a reward, or rewards.

H. So we need cooperative behavior which is the sacrifice of two or more persons to obtain a reward. Both of these people (or more, together cumulatively) will be sacrificing their time, effort, and knowledge (and sometimes their material) in an atmosphere of risk to produce either goods or services. So, cooperative behavior is two or more life entities adding together their time, effort, knowledge, and risk to attain a reward; and we make the sacrifices together to get the common reward because the participants perceive that the reward has goodness, thus, fulfilling Dictum 1 and Corollary 2.

D. And if allowed to do so, peace is prevalent.

H. Hence, I believe this brings this to the point of Corollary 4 which is that of cooperation.

D. Cooperative behavior is the sacrifice that individuals make in order to achieve a reward for each participant, and each participant has the additional knowledge that each participant will produce and receive a greater efficient goodness together than if alone.

H. And to produce cooperative behavior, knowledge that our sacrifice and our working together with other people will result in the greater ability to produce more goods and services with greater efficiency which will be good and which will allow us to live better is required. As a result we will consider others with whom we cooperate important to our lives; and thus, we will make instruments of cooperation, such as agreements, covenants, contracts. Examples of these types of agreements or contracts would be individuals with individuals; companies with companies; and society with government. We have already pointed this out when you were defining free-market enterprise.

D. I think it best to point it out again as these concepts are involved in the nature of understanding peace.

H. Ok.

D. There is a byproduct of societal freedom (which would be Corollary 1) and that is the convergence of priorities; that is, others may come to have the same priorities which is the nature of competition. Competition emerges through the convergence of priorities. That is, it naturally emerges from two factors: One, from the existence of freedom; and two, from St. Augustine's principle of Libido Dominandi (the lust for dominion; the desire to dominate); and this is Corollary 5.

H. So competition, which is produced by converging priorities, initiates the potential for war. To avoid economic war, companies attempt to diversify, such as, by adding or subtracting features, by lowering their prices, et cetera, which is as per the Law of

Differentiation, Corollary 6. Countries will conform to the Law through the use of treaties and international agreements.

H. Wait! We're hashing out the nature of free-market enterprise which we just discussed!

D. That's right we are. Peace is when society allows the procession of free-market enterprise to proceed.

H. But the inclusion of competition increases the potential for economic war which is the opposite of peace.

D. There is a reason why we have to include this principle (Corollary 5) into the nature of peace even though competition is the convergence of priorities and converging priorities are inimical to the health of the life entity. All companies, individuals, societies know that direct competition can take away from available resources. In the economic arena, it makes it harder to get customers. It's competition, which is produced by converging priorities, that initiates the potential for conflict as you correctly pointed out. Economic competition is essentially economic war and companies attempt to avoid this war by diversifying their products which is as per the Law of Differentiation (Corollary 6). But because of the Law of Differentiation, all is well within society, if there is freedom, as it allows the participants to avoid direct competition and proceed peacefully in the production of goods and services. As a result, overall, peace reigns.

H. Interesting.

D. Competition exists because within human nature there is this will to compete which evolved within the human species, as Saint Augustine noted in his book, City of God, and deemed it the principle of the Libido Dominandi.

H. And so, Corollary 5 is the concept of competition that equals the convergence of priorities by two or more entities. Corollary 6 is the Law of Differentiation which equals the divergence from the market priorities fulfilling new demand to deliver new products and services. All life knows that direct competition is inimical to one's health, and so it attempts to diverge away through differentiation. This law produces the variations of products in the marketplace.

D. Countries will conform to the Law of Differentiation through the use of treaties, and treaties are agreements that make cooperation, and thus peace, possible. Therefore, peace equals pursuance of Dictum 1. Peace resides within goodness and the good is within Dictum 1 which contains freedom which is Corollary 1 plus our equation of the Sacrifice equalling the Reward which is Corollary 2. Then, we add motivation which is the Sacrifice relative to the Reward which is Corollary 3 plus cooperation (Corollary 4) plus competition (Corollary 5) and the Law of Differentiation (Corollary 6).

H. Thus, peace is synonymous with the individual pursuance of that which is good.

D. And so, interdiction of any of the seeking of that which is good and of the constituent Corollaries will cause the potential for conflict, strife, and war to emerge.

H. Let's go through the Corollaries one by one.

D. Corollary 1 is freedom the interdiction of which has the potential to cause war because one of its possible causes are anti-knowledge which are rules and regulations of which one example would be heavy taxation. Corollary 2 is the introduction of our sacrifices to obtain a reward; and Corollary 3 is inclusive of our motivation to achieve the receiving of rewards. Corollary 4 would be the introduction of cooperative contracts, agreements, and covenants; and, when agreement and contracts are nonexistent or where they have been broken, cooperation is no longer possible. When cooperation disappears, then respect also vanishes and so does ethics.

H. Yes, if there are no ethics, then all that remains is the end justifies the means rationality. This is because, as we should remember, ethics is the appropriate dispensation of respect, and we respect others in order to facilitate cooperation, and we cooperate in order to produce goods and services which brings this up away from misery which is the essence of that which is good.

D. If we add in a situation of high motivation of a small sacrifice versus a great reward along with a convergence of priorities, the result is a high propensity for economic war.

H. And Corollary 5 is the concept of Competition which is the convergence of priorities that, as we have noted before, creates an ongoing basis for economic war.

D. In an extreme situation, competition can produce political war also. Corollary 6 introduces the Law of Differentiation and interdiction of this Law will cause the prospect for war to appear.

H. Thus, to summarize, when cooperation is destroyed with its attendant instruments of contracts, agreements, to the extent that there is not a possibility of Dictum 1 to be pursued, and only physicality, competition, non-divergence, and the principle of Libido Dominandi remain, then war is to be expected.

Chapter 7: The Nature of Violence

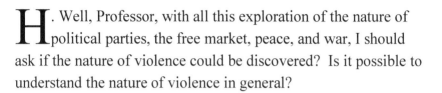

H. Well, Professor, with all this exploration of the nature of political parties, the free market, peace, and war, I should ask if the nature of violence could be discovered? Is it possible to understand the nature of violence in general?

D. Yes.

H. That would be remarkable. So, to that end, what is the nature of violence? There are so many causes, so many instances ranging from individual criminals to gangs, to the violence of pogroms and war. Is there a common thread that could lead us to an essence of violence?

D. Yes. There are two sources of the nature of violence. First is the adherence to the Dictums of the Haves along with adherence to Corollaries one to four by the perpetrator of violence. Secondly, violence can be initiated by the violation of the first principle of life by another. This observance of the Dictums of the Haves leads to the proclivity for violence and war along with a motivation supplied by the ratio of the perceived, potential sacrifice of implementing violence relative to the receiving of a reward (Corollary 3); and the natural rationale for violence in the case for self-defense would be caused by the interdiction of the Have-Not Dictums along with the six Corollaries of peace.

H. OK, please elaborate.

D. Every instance of violence from the myriad and severe wars caused by the royalty of the Haves down to violence caused by the

123

common street criminal can be understood and traced to adherence to the Dictums of the Haves and particularly to the violation of the first Dictum along with the Corollaries.

H. OK, let's go through this. How about the instance of the royalty of the Haves with all the wars they have created and caused throughout the thousands of years extending up to the last century which produced the most catastrophic killing of millions with, I am sure, more to come.

D. Wars of the Royal-Haves are caused by adherance to the Dictums of the Haves and a favorable adherence to any of Corollaries one to four. And the violation of any or all of the Have-Not Dictums and Corollaries would produce a revolution or rebellion.

H. Let's take the complicated example of the invasion of England at the Battle of Hastings in 1066 by William the Conqueror.

D. William's point of view was that he was originally promised the Crown by Edward, but in the end, it was given to Harold (Edward's son). This breach made William a Have-Not temporarily; and so for William (Edward's cousin), this was a violation of the Dictums of the Have-Nots, specifically 1, 2, 3, 4, 5, 6, & 7, while there is an adherence by William to the Have-Dictums as truly he is a Have.

H. I see that it is a violation of Dictum 1. William was prevented from becoming the King of England which is obviously an interdiction of William's seeking that which is good for him as Harold asserted his dominance in the matter as per Dictum 2. And, I can see that William's gathering a force to invade and causing the Battle of Hastings is in accordance with William's Dictum 2 which states that there is a human trait that causes men throughout the world to dominate.

D. Edward and/or Harold must have viewed William, for whatever reason, as bad and not the right choice for England as per Dictum 3. Further, William, also being a Have, would view the court of England as being inherently not good, Dictum 3. Next, as per Dictum 4, he would be of the opinion that there was an agreement in place with King Edward, and this had been violated because he, William, should have received the crown (making William a Have-Not); and ergo, the ethic of Have-Not Dictum 6 and the cooperative understanding of Corollary 4 had been breached, and accordingly, William examined the sacrifice relative to the reward which indicated to him a positive motivational situation (Corollary 3), and thus, he would be free to proceed in rectifying the situation by invading to seek the English Crown.

H. How about the creation and expansion of the Roman Empire which would involve the Have-Dictums for the advent of the wars and the Have-Not Dictums for the benefits that came to the expanding empire?

D. The wars of the Roman Empire would be in adherence to all the Dictums of the Haves: the Roman royalty and their facilitators, the Roman legions, were seeking that which was good for them, Dictum 1; Saint Augustine's principle is clearly in play; the Have-Nots would be seen as inherently not good, and so, the Roman Legions would bring good to the hinterlands, Have-Dictum 3; there is no contract in place between the Roman royalty and the people of the lands that were to be conquered, violating Have-Dictum 4 and Corollary 4; and as such, the Have-Not Dictum 6 whereby ethics is the appropriate dispensation of respect is not in place allowing the perpetration of the end justifies the means to be put in place, which is Dictum 6 of the Haves (in this situation of the Roman royalty). Lastly, the motivational ratio within Dictum 1 and Corollary 3 is positive as the added lands from afar would bring more tribute to be split between the local Roman rulers, the Roman Legion, and of course with the Royalty at Rome who don't have to do the fighting thereby making the motivational equation sufficiently inviting.

H. How about one more example; how about World War II?

D. This military action of Japan fulfilled the Dictums of the Haves of the Japanese Imperial Military inducing the propensity for war. First, it fulfilled their Dictums 1 & 2. The Japanese viewed the U.S. as bad for several reasons, such as inhibiting their acquisitional needs for oil, Dictum 3, thus probably adding to the Japanese point of view that military action would be self-defensive (at least partially) due to the U.S. violating the Japanese need for oil, and Corollaries 4 & 6 - Cooperation and Differentiation. There is no contract in place, Dictum 4. The Lord Acton Principle is at work as Japan was essentially a feudal nation, and as such, it was fully controlled by the Japan Imperial Haves, Dictum 5; consequently, its ethics is the ends justifies the means, Haves-Dictum 6; and as such, the Japanese Imperial Haves would have been fully susceptible to the propensity to commit war.

H. Yes, it fits.

D. For the U.S. part, leaving aside the McCollum Memorandum and the possibility that President Roosevelt, desiring the U.S. to join the effort in Europe, enticed Japan to start a war in the Pacific theatre through the promotion of the eight actions noted in the Memo, Japan did attack at Pearl Harbor thereby offending the sensibilities (Have-Not Dictum 6) of the U.S. political body allowing for the reaction to go to war. So first, the U.S. reaction

126

fulfilled Dictum 1 in its defense of itself which would be doing that which is good for itself, and fighting back would be fulfilling Libido Dominandi, Dictum 2; the Japanese act of war violates the Have-Not Dictums 1, 3, & 6 and Corollary 4, indicating that the others (the Japanese) are inherently not good and non-cooperative; and after the attack, doing good would be difficult because the adversary intends on prosecuting military victory which is a violation of the Have-Not Dictums 1, 3, 4, & 6, it also would be impossible to generate ethical cooperation which produces goodness at this point due to the violence committed (Dictum 6); and finally, the U.S. Have-Nots are prevented from seeking liberty, a violation of the Have-Nots Dictum 7.

H. Overall, the Japanese Imperial Government Haves would be adhering to the Dictums of the Haves which would give them the predilection of committing to war as history has shown us as being the habit of the Haves throughout the centuries.

D. The Japanese Haves, naturally, would follow Dictums 1 & 2; the Japanese would fulfill Dictum 3 of the Haves noting that America's nature is bad probably for several reasons; Dictum 5 would be applicable as Japan was controlled by a cadre of Haves thus making their outlook corrupt; ergo the military action by the Japanese at Pearl Harbor was as per Have-Dictum 6, destroying the ethics of cooperation thus initiating the end justifies the means mentality; therefore, with the abolition of ethical obligations (Dictum 6, Corollary 4), violence was easily induced by the sacrifice of military action given a motivation equation and adequate stock of Have-Not soldiers which are expendable (Have-Dictums 3 & 4 along with Corollary 3).

H. So, we might conclude that all the wars (not the revolutions) throughout history were started by a king or queen, despot, supreme leader, or cadre of Highnesses fulfilling one or more Dictums of the Haves along with sufficient motivation as per Dictum 1, Corollary 3.

D. Yes, Dictum 1 is fulfilled by the establishment of a priority of something that the potentate feels is good for himself and his domain which he considers as his possession through the corruption process in Have-Dictum 5, such as, to acquire more land or resources for his domain. This would probably run into a priority of another despot who considers the targeted area his alone; and thus, the convergence of priorities proceeds, which is competition (Corollary 5), which is inimical to the health of the competitors.

H. But really, the motivational ratio seems to not be consistent with a starting cause of the violence of war. I understand the king and queen would desire to acquire more goodness and one way to receive that goodness is to acquire more land, which will come with more proletariats to farm the land and give tribute, or more raw land into which the nobles and facilitators may move to expand their holdings and become wealthier. I understand that acquisition; but it comes at a high price if war is what it takes to make the acquisition because the royals will need an army to fight the war and with the violence of it comes a lot of death. So, when one examines the motivational ratio in order to construct a priority as to whether to go to war to acquire more territory, one would see a huge cost both in human terms and economic resources. As such, I am surprised it happens at all.

D. It happens, and it happens a-lot because of the fulfillment of all the Dictums, namely, Dictums 1, 2, 3, 4, 5, 6, & 7 of the Haves, in addition to the motivational ratio which is not as severe in the mind of the despot as one would think. The royal Haves do not do the fighting; their lives are not at stake; only their conscripted military slaves which come out of the Have-Nots are at risk. And when they are in surplus, they become easily expendable because they are of the Have-Not class; and as such, due to Dictum 3, they are looked down upon as these Have-Nots are inherently not good; the Have-Not soldiers are paid a small pittance satisfying Dictum 4 of Noblesse Oblige; Have-Dictum 5 begets the observance that the Have-Nots are not of consequence and expendable anyway as there is no obligatory need for cooperation, and because the minds of the Royalty become corrupted due to their absolute power; as such, Have-Dictum 6 is invoked as it is the result that the acquisition of wealth that is most important, not ethical behavior because the end justifies the means; and we should make mention of the additional justification that is our nature to dominate and compete (Dictum 2). Lastly, in order to accomplish all of this, Have-Dictum 7 is involved because the Haves always seek control of others which is a prioritized desideratum which enables the Haves to accept the risk noted in the motivational ratio.

H. I see. The motivation is that there is little risk because usually their lives are not at risk, and in the balance, there is a huge reward that may accrue to the fulfillment of their priorities and objectives of personal power and their ideology. Examples of ideological control would be Hitler with his fulfillment of expanding the area of Germany's influence and power along with his horrendous racial and cultural problematic objectives. More examples are Stalin along with Mao, Pol Pot, Castro, and others with their priorities of communist ideological purity causing their pogroms (Dictums 5, 6, 7) which allow for the corruption of their minds as these rulers did not have to cooperate with anybody allowing them to escape from any ethical considerations employing only the end justifies the means mentality in order to effectuate control over their respective societies.

D. Exactly. In the first case, all wars and their incumbent violence throughout history are fermented as per the fulfillment of the seven Dictums of the Haves. The more the seven Dicta of the Haves along with Corollary 3 (motivation) are fulfilled, the greater the propensity for war accrues. Secondly, the interdiction of Dictum 1 and the 6 Corollaries of peace (and/or the elements of free market enterprise) are the causes of the individual, group, or country to go to war on a self-defense basis.

H. Well, what about individual violence? We need to discuss violence committed by the single person, by private groups, such as gangsters, deranged men that commit mass shootings, the common criminal, and others that seem to come out of the Have-Not group predominantly.

D. The same Dictums apply and are to be used to elucidate the perpetration of this violence.

H. OK, how about history's famous gangsters?

D. The gangster is no different from the royalty except to say that they emanate from the Have-Not class, graduate to the middle class through their illegal activities and attempt to infiltrate the facilitator class of the Haves as the opportunity arises even though the two groups (the gangsters and the governmental facilitators) clash and are fierce competitors.

H. Is there a hybrid class that consists of both the Haves and the Have-Nots?

D. The overall defining characteristic to define how one person or group is of the Haves or the Have-Nots or has the potential to cause war or violence is the gradation of the amount of control that is dispensed. Both groups are, first, subject, as we all are, to the first Dictum of the Law of Demand for the Good. Both seek, just like everybody else, goodness for themselves, their families, and for their racketeering groups; and for those people or organizations that interrupt this objective of the Haves, or the Have-Nots, violence becomes a possibility. Both groups invoke Dictum 2 in trying to dominate each other and in doing so are often met with violence. As for the rest of the Dicta, as you take on the characteristics of the seven political behavioral principles of the Haves that we have delineated, that person or group will acquire a greater affinity toward control, and a propensity toward violence, irrespective of which class from which one might emanate, will grow. Remember: the class membership has some fluidity to it depending on the amount of control that is established within any society. Thus, in a totalitarian country that has established a total command control royal echelon, an interchange between the classes would be nil. In this case, the only chance for fluidity is probably through the recognition of mental or physical brilliance of an individual that could be seen by the Rightly-Guided Haves as being helpful to their priorities. In a non-command control society where freedom is the priority and control is less, there will be less propensity by the members of the government to seek war or make violence. As a rule, any group or individual will develop the affinity or propensity to violence as it takes on the characteristics of the seven principles of the Haves along with the circumstances of a propitious motivational ratio. As an example, let's look at Europe (and the rest of the world) whose history consists entirely of one district of the Haves committing violence on another area of the Haves or Have-Nots.

H. So, really the more any individual or government takes on the

131

characteristics of the Haves (which is to control), the more the propensity for violence arises.

D. Yes.

H. So, let's have another example. Let's consider the racketeering groups that throughout their history are given to violence.

D. They are, like everybody, subject to Dicta 1 & 2; the racketeering gangster would consider others outside their group as having priorities that are inherently not good (Have-Not Dictum 3); they would be strict observers of Dictum 4 in that they would have an obligation to assist cooperative adherents to those within their group. Consequently, they would seek to install a code of silence when speaking with outsiders and a conformity to a code of ethics for those inside the group (Dictum 6 of the Have-Nots would call for respect of the members with whom the members should cooperate); and for non-cooperative competitors outside their group they would follow Dictum 6 of the Haves (that the end justifies the means); and lastly, the gangster in their racketeering business dealings would follow Dictums 2 & 7 of the Haves in that they would seek control of others in their business developments. Violation of these Dicta would result in violence given an acceptable motivational reward ratio.

H. This would be compatible with zoological-anthropological theory. The zoologist, Desmond Morris, pointed out that humans have evolved the behavior of cooperative attitude amongst themselves when confronting threats to the group's exterior environment (Dictums 1 & 4 of the Have-Nots because within themselves they are at peace (under ideal circumstances)) and a will toward competitiveness (as per Libido Dominandi) when dealing with internal tribulations.

D. Again, there is a sense of obligation to take care of the gang members and their families (Dictum 4 of the Haves and Dictum 6 of the Haven-Nots); naturally, their power with which they deal with internal and external problems can corrupt their will to cooperate (Dictum 5 of the Haves), thus leading to violence outside their group causing their perception of the motivational ratio equation to become lowered and out of proportion when deciding whether to proceed with acts of violence, propelling them to believe that the end justifies the means when dealing with an external threat and ethical when dealing with internal cooperative gang members. Thus, the Boss-Haves seek control of their group members while seeking liberty for themselves to pursue their racketeering objectives, as per Dictum 7 of the Haves.

H. Let's move to the example of a common criminal who walks into a grocery store or convenience store to rob the proprietor of his money and in doing so causes the potential for violence to occur. I can see that Dictum 1, of course, comes into play because of the Law of the Demand for the good: the criminal will see that if he robs the convenience store, he will gain some cash which will help him with his daily needs in life.

D. He will have the will to dominate his adversary inside the store (Dictum 2); he will consider his adversary inherently not good (Dictum 3 of the Haves); being a conforming Have-Not, he will consider that Have Dictum 4 has been broken and society no longer is supporting him, and therefore, Noblesse Oblige has been violated; because this societal contract has been broken, he will in his mind believe that the will to cooperate is no longer there as for the temporary time of the robbery he converts to a Have, and so, his decisional capabilities are corrupted which would be Dictum 5 of the Haves. With no longer a need for cooperation within society, his ethics will now become the rationale of control which is that the end justifies the means. Therefore, his motivational equation will become skewed leading him to believe that his sacrifice is well worth the reward, and any intervention to this cause of obtaining the good within the cash register (Dicta 1 & 7 of the Haves) will produce a reaction of violence from the perpetrator who is temporarily a Have.

H. What about the mass shooter of which there seem to be two types: there is the ideological type such as the terrorist harboring a vision of Islamic Nirvana and there are those where no ideological objectives seem to be present. They slaughter just for the sake of killing.

D. The seven Dictums still apply; and let's go through them again to understand the answer to this question, first for the ideologically driven terrorist.

H. Naturally, Dictum 1 applies as there is no exception to this.

D. The terrorist will also want to dominate others as he will want to extend his ideology to others as his ideology is a screed that dictates how others should live (Dictum 1 & 2); and if terror assists in this endeavor, then he will employ it because of all Dictums of the Haves. Those who do not have a commensurate belief in the terrorist's ideals will be inherently bad in the eyes of the terrorist (Have Dictum 3). He will consider it obligatory to spread his ideology by force if necessary, especially if the ideology (such as Koran Sura 9, Verse 5, "then slay the idolaters wherever you find them" amongst many others) denotes specifically to do so (Have Dictum 4 for control through contract). His fervent belief in the screed will corrupt his mind into the belief that cooperation is not important when dealing with those non-believers in the ideology (Have Dictum 5, The Rationale of Non-

Cooperation); and thus, ethical behavior is discarded setting up his righteous belief that the end justifies the means (Have Dictum 6, the Rationale of Control and in this case the scripture itself may confirm this, such as Sura 8, Verse 65, "O Prophet, exhort the believers to fight…"); and ergo, Dictum 7 of the Haves, that further control through the violence of terror is fulfilled. Finally, the motivational equation and ratio of Dictum 1 are set up indicating to the terrorist that the sacrifice of violence is to be initiated as the reward of the spreading of his ideology is worth it (and again, the ideology may provide this motivation as per Sura 9, Verse 88, "But the Messenger, and those who believe with him, strive and fight with their wealth and their persons: for them are (asked) good things: and it is they who will prosper"); and as per Dictum 2, he will want his ideology to dominate.

H. How about the single mass shooter who has no motivational ideology that propels him to initiate his violent, senseless slaughter? There seems to be a growing number and frequency of these here in the United States.

D. The answer will require some speculation, but our method will lead us to as close an answer as the available information will allow.

H. Well, then, Dictum 1 will be in place as the killer will for some unknown reason believe that the killing action will accrue to his benefit. Obviously, he will experience Saint Augustine's principle of domination, and he will consider others as not being good, or should I say, in his mind as having no worth. But at this point, I am unsure about Dictum 4.

D. Have Dictum 4 is present in that he moves at least temporarily to the half side of the spectrum of control. The perpetrator of violence believes that society, or even his family, has broken his contract with him. The ideologically devoid murderer will feel that there is a contract or agreement in place and that others in his social environment have broken it. It may be that the elimination or violation of the agreement has caused him pain, mentally or physically, and thus, the pain and suffering of others in society is owed to him as just rectification of the broken agreement. The nature of the agreement would be (and we are speculating here as to what could be going on in his mind) that his society such as his parents, teachers, friends, all owe him a reasonable living, and he owes them to be a good kid, to grow up, be a decent, responsible adult, and also create a family; but somehow this agreement has been disrupted, and he's no longer obligated to his end of the bargain for whatever reason; and as a result, he may feel he is free to punish the other parties to the agreement, and he sets up his demented sacrificial reward equation ratio as he moves temporarily to the Haves.

H. I have a new hypothesis as to one way this could happen in some cases. I suspect that society puts into him some prescription drugs to moderate or change his behavior, and upon its conclusion, he suffers a depression or reaction to his withdrawal leaving him totally distraught and setting up the motivation to commit violence upon others, himself, or both. This would involve Dictums 1, 3, 4, 5, 6 & 7 of the Haves. The operation of these Dictums of societal action upon the perpetrator along with the motivational ratio would be the reason for his deployment of death since his mind becomes corrupted by the ingesting of drugs, by the withdrawal from the psychotropic medicines, or by other influences that are rampant in our society causing the demented killer to lash out with violent destruction upon others which is the ultimate form of control, fulfilling the Have-Dictum 7.

D. Interesting hypothesis.

H. So, is it that as the more an individual or group takes on the characteristics of being a Have, does it necessarily follow - given a conducive motivational ratio - that violence will follow? It does not seem to be feasible. It seems from all this that being a Have, or a person or group that has some of the characteristics of the Haves, would be given to violence under the circumstance of an appropriate motivational ratio. It further seems that we could just conclude that the Haves are bad people given to unethical actions with a propensity to violence. It seems that you are placing all the blame on the Haves for committing violence in society. So, I must ask you whether you have to be a Have in order to perpetuate violence? Is it that only the Haves commit violence or war? I find it hard to believe! I, of course, watch some news on TV and on the Internet, and I am seeing that there are both Haves and Have-Nots who have committed violence. Pray tell, is there an explanation for this phenomenon? How do we integrate this problem into all that we have discussed in this interview?

D. Violence has two sources. First, violence is a violation of the Dictums of the Have-Nots. This violation along with the motivational ratio is what causes violence for the Have-Nots. It is essentially the situation of self-defense. Self-defense can be at the personal level: individual versus individual; or it can be at the societal level in which case it could be a revolution. The second source is the fulfillment of the Dicta of the Haves, along with a preponderant fulfillment of the motivational ratio of Dictum 1 which will induce the Have to seek achievement of his goals (Dictum 1) through any means necessary (Dictum 6), and sometimes these goals will require violence in order to achieve them.

H. Well, the first two principles are the same for the Haves and the Have-Nots, so I can see that part.

D. The third and sixth Dictums of the Have-Nots, which are the rationales to cooperate and be ethical, say that Have-Nots see other people as being essentially good in nature and ethical; and as such, they are always willing to cooperate, compromise, and understand, if possible, the other's point of view and opinions. The ability to cooperate is key in the production of goodness. We cooperate in order to produce goods and services which brings us up away from misery which is the essence of the good. Extensive violation of these two Dictums by itself could bring on violence if the motivational equation is strong enough to produce an incentive to reap the rewards for violence if we are not able to cooperate. Violation of Dictum 3 of the Have-Nots could be caused by Dicta 3 and 5 of the Haves. Dictum 5 of the Have-Nots is the imperative to do good. We must help others because it is ethical to do so. There is a duty to be charitable.

H. The Bible teaches to do that and the Old Testament even tells us that we should tithe our earnings giving this portion to charity, temple, or to church which should do charitable things throughout the world. However, it doesn't seem to be that the violation of this Dictum would ever generate much violence. I don't see that it would be able to initiate a motivational equation ratio strong enough to provoke someone to violence. It just seems unlikely.

D. Yes, you're probably right about that. Dictum 4 of the Have-Nots is the rationale that freedom is essential for society. It says that absolute freedom begets ethicalities absolutely. In other words, the freedom noted in Dictum 1, that all life pursues that which is good for it, tells us to use our freedom to pursue the cooperative situation that promotes goodness in our lives.

Cooperation allows us to pursue production of goods and services which brings us up away from misery about which we just spoke a little bit ago. So, the more freedom we have in society, the more cooperation, the more respectful ethical behavior, and the more likely that goods and services that bring goodness to our lives will be promoted and proliferate throughout our societal environment.

H. Yes, I can see that. We know that ethics is the appropriate dispensation of respect and respect is the evolutionary characteristic that enables us to cooperate, and we cooperate in order to produce goods and services which brings us up away from misery which is the nature of all that is good which is Dictum 6.

D. And if there is a disruption of our ethical sensibilities in the ability to cooperate and respect others, this could cause violence given the motivation. We all want to produce that which is good for us, and the interruption of that can cause violence if there is in accompaniment the appropriate motivational equational ratio which is the essence of self-defense.

H. I agree. If you take away societal freedom, people will become unhappy because they will not be able to attain the goodness that they seek in their lives. The more you take away freedom, the more unhappy they will all be. But why? Why is it necessarily so that the absence of freedom will produce the potential for violence?

D. Let's recall the essence of freedom: it is the cerebral creation of a priority and then the effectuation of the priority into reality. These priorities are the seeking of that which is perceived by the individual to be that which is good for us. If in this process of seeking good for us there is interdiction of the production of the priorities and/or their effectuations, then less goodness is produced; and the interdiction of the first principle of life occurs which is Dictum 1. As a result, the individual will necessarily become unhappy with the diminished production of goodness for himself. As the interdiction of the production of goodness increases, the more the individual will be dissatisfied with his production of goodness and will necessarily become unhappy. If the unhappiness keeps increasing, there will be a point where the individual will consider that the motivational ratio may well produce a reward relative to the sacrifice that could begin to direct the unhappy individual toward the world of violence.

H. I see.

D. The means to this interdiction of the production of goodness by the Have-Nots is control induced by the Haves.

H. Control is the supplanting by force another's priorities with the priorities of oneself, and thus, is it that we could say that control is a negative sacrifice?

D. Correct, and we should recall that a sacrifice is one's risk, knowledge, time, effort, and material. Therefore, a negative sacrifice would be an anti-effort variable along with a new knowledge priority from another life entity, and this new sacrifice with its superior amount of anti-effort supplants the original priorities of the individual seeking out that which is good for him.

H. I see. As this control grows, so correspondingly the unhappiness of the individual life entity, which is the object of the control, increases.

D. Yes.

H. Would it be possible to summarize the will to violence? The aforementioned discussion was pretty complicated.

D. When one adheres to the Have-Dictums 1 through 7, the propensity to foment war arises. History indicates that it doesn't necessarily occur, but the probability rises. As such, the Haves have caused the initiation of wars and conflicts throughout history.

H. And the Leftist-Haves are still at it in recent history, and predictably they will cause more in the future.

D. A second type of war is the revolution or rebellion caused by the oppression of the the Haven-Nots by the Haves adhering to their Dictums in contravention to the Dictums of the Have-Nots. The Leftist-Haves paranoid of this possibility constantly work to keep weapons out of the reach of the Have-Nots.

H. And oppression is the forceful usurpation of the priorities of the Have-Nots with the priorities of the Haves that are generated inside Dictum 1 which is that all life does that which is good for it on an ongoing basis.

D. The third case is the one of self-defense which is similar to the rebellion. It is essentially the interdiction of Dictum 1 along with the violation of the Corollaries of peace resulting in a loss of freedom. As such, when nations, societies, or individuals being at peace (Dictum 1 + the Corollaries), become subject to outside aggression, which is the will or action of the interdiction of one's own priorities by the control of another (the will to control), then the reaction of self-defense may occur depending on the extent of the interdiction of Dictum 1 and the violation of the Corollaries. If the interdiction of Dictum 1 of an entity is not of the extent that changes the position of its Corollaries (which could be put to a graph) to too great an amount, then perhaps an accommodation can be made by the entity. But if the position of Dictum 1 and its

Corollaries are moved beyond a point of tolerance as dictated by its own priorities, then a violent reaction in the form of self-defense could result.

H. But something is incomplete in this discussion of the rebellion or revolution of the Have-Nots. Just the violation of the Have-Not Dictums do not produce the violence of the revolutions of history. Sometimes, they are horribly violent. Let's take an example: the first French revolution that produced the Reign of Terror. Violation of the seven Dictums of the Have-Nots did not cause the Jacobins' atrocities.

D. Yes, good point.

H. What then is the explanation?

D. Upon an ever greater intrusive interdiction of the Have-Not Dictums by the Haves, a point is exceeded, and the Have-Nots explode and become the Haves.

H. What?

D. Just as we discussed before whereby the individual robber-thief comes out of his conforming class of being of the Noblesse Oblige Dictum 4 to enter temporarily the class of the Haves to commit his robbery, the violated Have-Nots come out of their serf, proletariat, slave classes to enter temporarily (or permanently) the class of the Haves employing the seven Dictums of the Haves to forsake intellectual debate and discussion to seek the use of violence to effectuate their objective of bringing freedom to society.

H. I see. They look to the Have-Dictum 6 and utilize the thought that might makes right, as now, the end justifies the means.

D. And the result was the Reign of Terror.

H. At this point, I should ask, are they no better than their former oppressors? They have become just as all the Haves were throughout history, causing all the wars and man's inhumanity to man. What are we to think?

D. There are two resultant contingencies that have occurred in history that arise from the violent rebellion of the overthrow of an oppressive regime. First possibility is that rebels replace the oppressors with their own version of oppression and become another version of the oppressive Haves. The second solution is that these temporary Haves, upon conclusion of the revolt, revert to being the Have-Nots setting up a new form of government that adheres to the seven principles of the Have-Nots.

H. Got it! Such as the American revolution whereby the Founding Fathers set up a government consisting of our Constitution with the Bill of Rights that adheres to the seven Dictums of the Have-Nots.

D. Right.

H. OK, but one more question. During the interim period of rebellion whereby there is bloodshed, can there be adherence to the ethicalities noted in the Have-Not Dictums 4, 5, & 6? In other words, can a violent rebellion or revolution be ethical? Further to the point, could a deadly response whereby a person using self-defense such as the store clerk against a perpetrator be deadly yet

143

still remain ethical and as such be seen as a good actor?

D. Definitely, yes.

H. What is the basis that we may come to such a conclusion?

D. All we need to do is examine the nature of ethics.

H. Ethics is the appropriate dispensation of respect. But how do we know what is appropriate?

D. We look to the agreements, contracts, or covenants that govern the cooperative relationship of the entities involved in the ethical situation to see if the parties have fulfilled the rights and obligations listed and understood to be present in the association.

H. Of course, I should have realized this. When one fulfills his obligations under the agreement, then one should receive the appropriate amount of respect which would be the fulfillment of the rights (enumerated, implied, written, verbal, or understood) declared in the agreement. Respect would be the behavioral actions inherent within the obligations and rights of an agreement.

D. Correct.

H. But once the hostilities of the rebellion begin, the contracts are obliterated, and the situation becomes devoid of ethics and irrelevant to the situation. So how can the revolt, or for that matter, any war, whether it is of a self-defensive nature or not, be justified and be understood as ethical?

D. It is due to the situation leading up to revolt. In pre-rebellion, the Haves reduced the rights of the Have-Nots because they are deplorable (Dictum 3) to a level whereby the lives of the Have-Nots are intolerable and thus the Have-Nots are not receiving any of the respect that is due to them creating an unethicality that is intolerable. The Haves have extracted the ethicalities in their relationship with the Have-Nots, and only an a-ethical situation results.

H. So all ethics have been depopulated from the relationship, and as such, the ethics are no longer relevant. Thus, I would imagine this would create a powder keg of a situation just waiting for the explosion; and the Haves would usually know this and accordingly try to prevent weapons from getting into the hands of the Haves-Nots as history has shown us that they are want to do.

D. Correct.

H. So the sense of ethics departs the scene, the Have-Nots rebel, the Have-Nots go over to employing the Dictums of the Haves, and bloodshed ensues. But still, is it right? Is it justified? Would Jesus approve? Can we, or should I say the Have-Nots, be morally OK to enter into bloodshed and violence of any type?

D. Yes, even in the Bible, as Jesus declared there is such a situation as in Matthew 7:12, which says as per the King James Version, "Therefore all things whatsoever ye would that men should do to you, do ye even so to them: for this is the law and the prophets."

H. Understood. If others have denuded a situation of any ethical considerations, then we may act appropriately.

D. That's how I read it. But it is incumbent upon the Have-Nots, upon conclusion of hostilities to return society to the observance of the Dictums of the Have-Nots and resume the ethicalities of freedom in order for the rebels to be righteous. Many times in history – especially recent history – whereby upon a successful rebellion, the former Have-Nots do not return to being the Have-Nots but become permanently within the realm of the Haves.

H. Good point! It seems that most of the time this is the case. Lenin, Mao, Castro to name a few exemplify this situation.

Only the American Revolution did not allow the employment of a new set of the Haves. I suppose the English revolution and the French revolutions also could qualify to be in this category; it just took them somewhat longer.

D. Right.

H. Well Professor, that was pretty interesting about the proclivity of the Haves to start wars; and it was also a particularly interesting statement to say that violence is the directional bias toward the principles of the Haves, and the opposite direction, which is in the direction toward the Dictums and Corollaries of the Have-Nots, which is the direction for self-defense, is toward peace.

D. Yes, it is a fascinating subject.

H. Well now, I have another particularly interesting question in its size and scope.

D. OK, let's hear it!

Chapter 8: The Rise & Fall of Empires

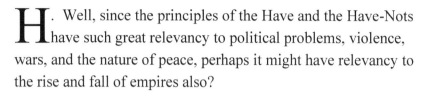

H. Well, since the principles of the Have and the Have-Nots have such great relevancy to political problems, violence, wars, and the nature of peace, perhaps it might have relevancy to the rise and fall of empires also?

D. Yes, it surely does.

H. Oh wow! Is it possible to explain such a concept? Please without ado.

D. It is just as it is with the commencement of war. The more an empire or civilization moves to embrace the principles of the Haves and away from being desirous to being adherent to the principles of the Have-Nots, the tendency to a downfall will proceed. In the opposite direction, should an empire, culture, or civilization hold dear the principles of the Have-Nots, there will be the Empire that prospers.

H. And why is that?

D. It is as we discussed previously: the more society, or in this case its civilization, moves toward the principles of the Haves, then the rate of the production of knowledge - and consequently the production of efficiencies - within society starts to decrease. Likewise in the opposite direction should a society or civilization move to uphold the principles of the Have-Nots, there, the production of knowledge and subsequently the efficiencies that may be brought into society and into an economy will be brought forth efficaciously. Further, the use of cooperative behavior will increase thereby facilitating the production of goods and services.

147

H. And would this directional bias within the production or adherence to the principles of the Haves and the Have-Nots be able to interpret the rise and fall of all great civilizations?

D. Indubitably.

H. Well how about the first and the greatest of these empires and civilizations which was the Roman Empire. How could these principles explain the rise and fall of the Roman Empire?

D. The reason why the Roman empire became successful was the implementation of Roman law which included motivation, contract law, property rights, and Roman citizenship. This provided greater opportunity for more people within the Roman Empire. As such, the production of knowledge increased throughout its citizenship and populace. It gave opportunity to the Have-Nots to become up out of the serfdom, slavery classes and jump up to the middle-class; and additionally Rome incentivized military class opportunity. It extended these attributes to the Roman legions and provided its soldiers the opportunity for the accumulation of assets upon serving in the Roman legions for the empire, thus producing an efficient army. These policies fulfilled the Have-Not Dictums 1, 3, 4, 5, 6, & 7.

H. Yes, interesting.

D. And the opposite was true in its downfall.

H. Yes. The incentives to provide opportunity for the soldiers to receive that what is good for them decreased, violating Dictum 1. Secondly, decadence began to beset the Rome aristocracy as per Dictum 5 of the Haves.

D. The English revolution was the same. Parliament wrested control from the royalty in 1688 and created the English Bill of Rights. This was a big step in the process of moving toward the principles of the Have-Nots, and as such, the Have-Nots obtained the opportunity to come out of the lower slave, proletariat class and move into a middle class fulfilling Have-Not Dictums 1, 3, 4, 5, 6, & 7. This process lasted until today. The British empire created a magnificent navy and enjoyed the industrial revolution, and this resulted in prosperity; but then it encountered the travesties of World Wars I & II.

H. Yes, World War I consisted of the machinations of all the political interests and treaties and agreements whereby a set of Haves colluded on one side and another side was organized by another set of Haves. It is unfortunate that the Haves brought misery and death to the Have-Nots who had to fight in the world wars that were created by the Haves. It was senseless to say the least. It is amazing: the power of Dictum 5!

D. So regarding the rise and fall of the British empire, it is as all the empires are or have been: during the rise, there is an accentuation of the adherence to the Dictums of the Have-Nots, and during a decline it is because that empire moves to the principles of the Haves. But with regards to the British empire, there really hasn't been a decline because it has been moving gradually little by little to the Dictums of the Have-Nots since the Magna Carta. Although geographically the empire shrunk lately, London has proliferated and become quite prosperous becoming the major financial center of Europe.

H. Yes, after World War II, Britain, along with other countries that had colonial empires, made a conscious policy decision to retract their influence from those colonies and center upon governance of their own countries only. They did this from international and internal pressure which indicated that these colonial powers had no right to be extraterritorial in their management of other countries.

D. Yes.

H. I have read that throughout history the rise and fall of empires seem to be cyclical, and in examining these occurrences, one might conclude that they are unavoidable and that they are fateful in that they will always eventually fail. In other words, when empires are on the rise, it necessarily means that someday the empire will necessarily fall. It is as if the fall of an empire is a fait d'accompli. Are empires doomed to fail?

D. Very interesting question.

H. Is the United States doomed to fall someday? And now that I am thinking about this, it seems the U.S. has already started to decline while simultaneously Asia seems to be on a trajectory of ascendance and will become the next empire. Are empires doomed to failure from the beginning? All of them throughout history have become decadent and eventually deteriorated. None has persisted and stayed successful. Professor, what do you think?

D. The answer is twofold: yes, almost all have failed. Initially, the empires start out by adhering to at least to some degree to the principles of the Have-Nots allowing the Have-Nots the opportunity to work themselves out of being slaves, giving them the chance of jumping out of the proletariat class, but eventually, the empires nullified those Have-Not principles and thus obliterated the opportunities, and as such, the once prosperous society began to deteriorate. Further, it is difficult to prevent the principles of the Have-Nots from being corrupted and becoming eventually the principles of the Haves.

150

H. How so?

D. We have already pointed out that Dictum 3 of the Have-Nots is that they see others in society to be generally of a good nature and the other person is assumed to be good until otherwise demonstrated as not good. Therefore, the Have-Not will assume that the ideas and actions of the other could be good and so the Have-Not will readily work to cooperate and compromise. If one holds the other to be bad, as the Haves do, one will resist cooperation and compromise thereby insuring that the ultimate goal of the Haves is not compromised.

H. Ok.

D. Dictums 4, 5, & 6 of the Have-Nots indicate that helping others should be voluntary; and when dispersing one's own resources in charity, one will work to see that the disbursement will be efficient. However, with Dictum 4 of the Haves, the royal, or that is, the governmental class will disburse the welfare, and it will not be done as efficiently because it is not coming out of one's own pocket but is of the OPM class, or that is, other people's money.

H. Yes, indeed.

D. When freedom in society is implemented as per Have-Not Dictums 4 & 5, then cooperation proliferates at maximum speed facilitating the construction and effectuation of priorities presenting societies with great efficiencies. Conversely, Dictum 5 of the Haves brings on greater centralized control of society inhibiting the creation of new knowledge and thus societal productive efficiencies.

H. Understood.

D. When the Have-Not Dictum 6 (The Essence of Ethics) is allowed, then the importance of the other person with whom one is dealing becomes paramount, and as such, respect becomes prevalent in society.

H. And as we have already established, respect is the essence of ethical behavior which is so important, obviously, in society. Respect allows us to cooperate together to produce that which is good for ourselves and by extension good for others also in society.

D. Ergo, freedom for society, Have-Not Dictum 7, is the most efficacious in producing goodness for society.

H. OK, I see that moving from the principles of the Have-Nots to the principles of the Haves will cause society eventually to decline. But still, is this rise and fall of an empire, or any society for that matter, an overwhelming societal tidal wave in that it cannot be stopped?

D. There is a tendency for societies to move to the principles of the Haves, and not only is it because of their Dictum 3 (The Rationale of Control), which we have discussed, but it is also because of Dictum 1 & 2 which describes why one will become a leader. As societies are constantly producing individuals who want to become a leader, there will be a tendency for society to move toward the principles of the Haves especially when considering Dictums 1, 2, & 3.

H. So, our society is also doomed? America is also headed for extinction?

D. The answer is a qualified no!

H. Oh, it is good news; but why not?

D. Because this society did something no other society has done before, except the English to some extent, and it guarantees the stubborn nature of the American society to continually stay with the principles of the Have-Nots and thus will continually enjoy prosperity unless some catastrophic outside events somehow interrupt it. The Founding Fathers had the wisdom to foresee this contingency, and thusly, inserted within the original fully ratified agreement between the people and the newly established government, the Bill of Rights which allows the principles of the Have-Nots to be preserved. Of particular importance are Amendments 4, 5, 9, 10, and subsequently, 14, 15, 19 along with Article 1, Section 10 of the Constitution.

H. Yes, I can see that Amendment 5 allows our seeking that which is good (Dictum 1), and I can see that all the Amendments, along with Article 1, Section 10 protect our freedom to create contracts that facilitate cooperation to produce goodness which is the purpose of Have-Not Dictums 3, 4, 5, 6 & Corollary 4; and they protect society and government to remain ethical and cooperative. All Amendments protect the ethics of Have-Not Dictum 6 and the seeking of liberty, Dictum 7.

D. These Have-Not Dictums are preserved through the Bill of Rights which protect the Have-Nots from the Leftist-Haves and its government facilitators who would come for everything if it were not for these restrictions on the Haves.

H. That is eminently true. When the the Haves get in control of the government, the first thing they do is attack any or all of the Bill of Rights and raise taxes and/or spend copious sums of money blurting out some sort of excuse to do so.

D. Exactly!

H. And so, as to the subject of whether the United States will be included in the rise and fall predictions in the future as other empires have been in the past, it seems there is a chance America has the potential to be the exception even though they all have fallen. But we've made a prediction that the United States could be the anomaly because it has enumerated rights of the people as denoted in the Bill of Rights, along with Article 1, Section 10 of the Constitution; and these are crucial to maintaining the freedom, prosperity, and opportunity of the Have-Nots. So my question here is if these Amendments are honored throughout history, then will it not follow that the United States will not fall and decline as other empires have done in the past?

D. The answer is unfortunately that it is not certain that it would be enough to prevent a downturn just as it is written and just as the amendments are. It would take one more amendment to secure the future of the United States.

H. Gosh! I don't see that happening anytime soon with the parties as divided as they are. Most of the Have-Not Republicans are hugely divided from the Leftist-Haves which we can call now the Democrats. So I don't think an additional amendment is in the cards in our near future. Certainly the Senate could come to no agreement, no matter whatever the amendment would be.

D. The only way to get through another amendment would be through a convention of the states.

H. Well, just for the sake of conversation, we're going to assume that it could happen through a states' convention. So assuming it is possible, what is the additional amendment that is needed in order to ensure our future and that this nation will not decline?

D. We have seen that throughout history that the Haves constantly spend too much due to their need to dole out largesse to their constituencies as per the Have-Dictums 1, 4, & 5. This is habitual and eventually they will overload the capacity of the U.S. economy. They will lead toward decadency, and as such, as it is with almost all previous empires, we will decline. The deficit spending will be aided by the propensity to print money by the central bank; and the only way to avoid this is to place upon the nation a balanced budget with a tax and debt limit amendment. Of course, there are times in extremis, such as upon a declaration of war, whereby the country will have an emergency need for money and the amendment would have to allow for such contingencies. But other than that, there needs to be such an amendment (or amendments) along the lines as discussed by Mark Levin in his book, *The Liberty Amendments*.

H. I agree.

D. There needs to be two parts as to the amendment. First one is to actually limit the fiscal budget of United States and its capacity to tax. Second part is to control the Federal Reserve Bank. We have seen in the past, and will see it again in the future, the zeal of the Federal Reserve to cooperate with the needs and desires of the politicians to print money to purchase the bonds created by the Treasury Department that's increasing the money supply at whatever rate for which they currently have need causing inflation and other monetary catastrophes. If they print too quickly and the amount is greater than the increase in productivity plus the GDP improvement year over year (assuming there are increases), that increase of the M2 money supply will cause inflation and become detrimental to society's creditors.

H. So, there are two parts for this: the first part is to prevent the United States government from borrowing too much money always having the financial ability to pay its creditors; and secondly, the federal reserve should not be allowed to print in excess of a certain amount each year.

D. The amount could be denoted as per a formula which would target a nominal inflation/deflation rate, such as, The RITE Report Inflation Index which is: Year over Year M2 money supply % increase, minus GDP, minus Productivity = The Index.

Chapter 9: The Rise & Fall of Companies

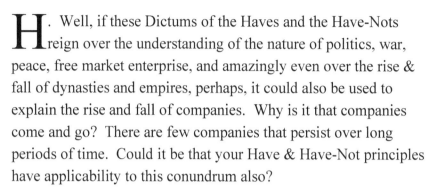

H. Well, if these Dictums of the Haves and the Have-Nots reign over the understanding of the nature of politics, war, peace, free market enterprise, and amazingly even over the rise & fall of dynasties and empires, perhaps, it could also be used to explain the rise and fall of companies. Why is it that companies come and go? There are few companies that persist over long periods of time. Could it be that your Have & Have-Not principles have applicability to this conundrum also?

D. They do, but modifications of our Dictums are required.

H. I would suppose that the rise of companies would be close to the Dictums of the Have-Nots and the fall of companies would be similar to the Dictums of the Haves. Dictums 1 & 2, I would suspect, would be as they are, without modification, as they appear to be universal for the Homo sapiens species.

D. Correct. Let's make a list. First is for the Have-Not company which is for the up and coming corporation.

Dictum 1: The Law of Demand for the Good - All companies do that which is good for it and continue to do that which is good for it on an ongoing basis.

Dictum 2: Saint Augustíne's Principle of Libido Dominandi - A company will have the will to compete and dominate.

Dictum 3: The Company's View of Competitors - Company's perspective of the marketplace is that the other companies are formidable competitors.

Dictum 4: The Necessity to Do Good - There is a necessity to produce goodness in the products and/or services in order to provide goodness for the customer, and consequently, profit for the corporation.

Dictum 5: The Law of Differentiation & Rationale of Efficiency - The company must constantly differentiate as per the demands of the competition, and as such, develop efficiencies to provide greater goodness in the company's products and services.

Dictum 6: Ethics - The company ethic is to respect its customers by providing the best goods and/or services possible.

And for the fall of companies, Dictums 1 & 2 are the same.

Dictum 3: The Company's View of Competitors - The company's view of the marketplace is that the competition is not so formidable and is of little concern.

Dictum 4: The Rationale of Corporate Control - The officers of the company will gain and consolidate its total control of the company away from the Board of Directors.

Dictum 5: Rationale of Corporate Corruption - The company officers will establish the priority of the company to be to provide goodness for the officers themselves first.

Dictum 6: Corporate Ethic - The company ethic will be to provide profit (goodness) for itself first before considering the goodness of the customer.

H. If I understand these Dictums correctly, they indicate that young companies with good products will establish an internal work ethic to develop efficiencies in their products which includes differentiation which promotes goodness within the company's production of its goods and services that it has for sale.

D. Correct.

H. And older, more mature companies, if they move away from the aforementioned Corporate Dictums of the Have-Nots, will experience the officers gaining total control while the board of directors become subservient to the officers (Dictums 2 & 4) and prioritizing the company policy to consider the goodness of the corporation first in its decisions instead of considering the goodness of the customers of the corporation as its prime objective.

D. This would typically be the result of the company prioritizing itself away from promoting the production of products and services to the priorities of the financial matters of the company.

H. I have read that historically there have been internal company struggles that occur between the founders' concerns with the company products and the views of the company CFOs; and I would predict that when a CFO gains control over a corporation, that company would begin its decline.

Chapter 10: Overview

H. Now that we have explained the origin of politics, the rise and fall of empires, the essence of the Free Market Enterprise System, and the other concepts such as peace & war, what do you suppose would be the perspectives of the Haves and the Have-Nots relative to these concepts as per their usefulness and efficacy, and secondly, would they (the Haves) be advocates for free market enterprise?

D. Well, it, of course, starts with our predecessors and the evolution allowing mankind to appear on this earth and become successful. We socially evolved from groups of Homo sapiens to tribes of Homo sapiens and then into super-tribes. Once we get to the level of the super-tribe, society brings out the characteristic of being impersonal whereby everybody no longer knows everybody else as pointed out again by Desmond Morris. As society becomes larger, the super-tribe groups, also known as classes, within society become impersonal, and there arises the awful super-tribe characteristic of man's inhumanity to man which is the result of Dictum 5.

H. Yes.

D. Concurrent to this is the principle of Libido Dominandi; and as such, there evolves the appearance of a tribal leader, and then there evolves a super-tribal leader also known as the king. Once we have a leader in place, we have the beginnings of the political party. And let's remember the definition of politics which is the polemics of how society should operate. But when this is combined with Dictums 1 & 2, we have now a political party that wants to or intends to rule society in the way that the king feels is best which includes Dictum 1 which is that all life does that which is good for it which in combination with Dictums 2 & 3 produces a tribal leader, and subsequently, a super-tribal leader, who would act upon society with the actions and policies that are good for that leader primarily with little reference to what is good for society as a whole. Add in Dictum 5 (the Lord Acton Principle), and ipso facto, in the mind of the leader, society's good, which is relative to the head of society (the leader, himself), will become the good of the state, and subsequently, the king will dictate the good of society.

H. Dangerous. Due to the corruption of the mind as per the Dictum 5 of the Haves, the will to dominate (and thus to compete) as per Dictum 2, and the principle that all life does that which is good for itself as per Dictum 1, there is a progression by the royalty of the Haves to believe that they are the state and what is good for them is also best as a policy for the proletariat. The dictate of "L'Etat, c'est moi" and the concept of the Divine Right of Kings indicate the ridiculous power of corruption of Dictum 5. Yet, my question still stands: would the Haves favor or disfavor inherently Free Market Enterprise?

D. No, they don't favor it at all. They only have use for the Free Market if it is within the confines of their upper-class camaraderie and only to the extent that they must pay bills, as even they have some bills to pay. As such, there are those with whom they must cooperate in order to accomplish the incorporation of their luxuries into their lives. Therefore, the royalty make allegiances with the nobles to assist with the administration of their lands and assets; and as the super-tribes grow, the nobles would require their functionaries to effectuate their policies which are to receive the confiscation of the labor of the slaves and the tribute, rents, taxes from the serfs. Any sense of the free market would only exist at the very highest level of society. There, between the royals and the nobles, could be a free market whereby there is a free buying and selling of the land and other possessions of the royalty and nobles between each other as per the freedom noted in their Dictums 1 & 6 because the societies of the royalty and nobles enjoy the Dicta of the Have-Nots for themselves only.

H. But the modern-day Haves of the democratic republics employ the free market for their entire society, I would think.

D. They do, here, only because they have no choice ... so far. Please note that their obstacle is the election process which slows down their progress of achieving the institution of their seven principles of political thought which, if allowed, would put society under their total control. With their Dictums in mind, they would move society toward the total control of the Have-Nots by the Haves.

H. And the Have-Nots? They would move in the opposite direction?

D. Given their seven Dicta, they would naturally be at peace which is the same thing as free-market capitalism. The Have-Nots will seek that which is good for themselves, and they recognize that societal liberty is the environment that allows them to seek the goodness that they desire.

H. OK, I now realize how to synthesize the concept of the seven principles of the Have-Nots with the other concepts which we discussed which were peace, war, and the free market. These explanations are all connected to the seven dictates through the portal of the first principle that all life seeks that which is good for it and is enabled to do so when there is liberty for all.

D. Yes.

H. Well, thank goodness for the wisdom of the Founding Fathers who recognized this and established the Constitution & the Bill of Rights which ensures freedom through their presence as the anti-government rules of the amendments allowed America to become the world's greatest nation as we previously pointed out.

D. Without the Bill of Rights, the Haves would make constant incursions into the Constitutionally ensured freedoms.

H. True. These incursions are constantly on display in the daily news where we see that the Haves try to take away the liberties of the Have-Nots by generating more laws and regulations against what the lower classes may do, destroying the freedoms of the Have-Nots.

D. There are three common ways that governments destroy societies. First way is through the continued assault upon a society by an ever piling on of the laws and regulations (which are elements of anti-knowledge) in order to effectuate further control as per all the Dicta of the Haves, but particularly through Dictum 7, destroying the creation of knowledge. The second way to destroy a society is through government fiat inflation generating an ever increasing amount of currency, then the government using that excess to purchase the goods and services of the society, per Dictums 1, 5, 6, & 7 of the Haves. The third way is for the government to over-spend causing excessive debt.

H. Yes, I think we have already discussed how the increase of control is inimical to any society. But just to review: as control increases, it, of course, brings with it anti-freedom. Anti-freedom brings the cessation of the effectuation of the priorities of the participants of a society. These individual priorities are replaced with the priorities of the government. Priorities are made up of knowledge and information. Thus, a generation of information by the many is replaced with the generation of information by the few that are within the government controlled by the Haves. As this replacement continues, the amount of knowledge being used within a society decreases because the number of sentient beings that holds the knowledge is being reduced; and as it is reduced, so is the amount of knowledge in society and so is the amount of knowledge being created for use by the government and society.

D. Right.

H. And you mentioned the second way a government can wreck a society is through the printing of money which means inflation. Many economists have written about this explaining how inflation will necessarily cause the destruction of society. Of course, the cost of goods and services increases as more money chases the same amount of products and services; and the main and customary cause of inflation is that the society's central bank will create greater currency amounts which will be greater than the growth of the economy. All money in any society must be backed by the production of goods and services of that society. If there's no production of goods and services, then money in that society will have no value: money represents that which a society produces. The government takes its printed dollars and buys goods and services. Further, this cheap money is available to the banks and other lenders through the central bank which buys the bonds of the various agencies of the government and the loans that were created by the banks. Of course, as a result of the extra money in society, the cheaper dollars are advantageous to the borrowers of society. Every economic text will tell you that the borrowers get to repay their loans with currency that is less expensive and less valuable because of inflation.

164

D. It is also advantageous to the government which borrows much of its money to pay for its spending on such things as welfare and other transfer payments. When this happens, the producers of society of the goods and services and the working people are essentially lending the value of their production to the government, and in a future exchange, they will receive value, but it will be less than the value that they loaned to the government in the first place to pay for its excess payments. Essentially, the people's value of its production of goods and services is being depreciated by the government's central bank as it essentially is borrowing and then paying back that value with money that is of lesser value. As the government borrows more and more from the people of society, the depreciation of the value of that which is produced by the society will eventually be overwhelming, and sadly, the society will go into depression.

H. Yes, inflation is well explained in economic textbooks, but I have never extrapolated the explanation to include the concept that the printing of money is the outright taking of the goods and services of the people by the government of the Haves. But the government is composed of the conservative Right which in America is supposedly the Republicans and the liberal progressive Left which is supposedly the Democrats, and according to what we have established in this conversation, both would be considered to be of the Haves and both being of the government. I say this because I know that sometimes there is little difference between the two parties. When together they go about spending way more than they should, sending the government into debt to an extent that is way more than is good for the nation. Nevertheless, it does seem to me that the Republicans seem to be slightly more fiscally responsible than the Democrats. This leads me to ask whether there is a reason for that?

D. Yes, there is. The Republicans are more solicitous of the principles of the Have-Nots, and the Democrats have the overt need to spend as much as they can.

H. How so?

D. We briefly touched upon this previously, but it is because of democracy and the progression of society to being knowledge-based. As we know from our review of *The Philosophical Equations of Economics* which states that the sacrifice equals a reward, and the major component that constantly is being added and injected into the equation is knowledge, and as knowledge grows in society, people become more important in that each individual becomes more able to bring efficiencies into the economy; and as such, individuals become more important to society, adding to the differentiation of society (as per the Law of Differentiation) and thus will more likely adhere to the principles of the Have-Nots, particularly to Have-Not Dictums 1, 4, 5, 6, & 7.

H. Right; and therefore, the Republican will gain voters as the Democrats will tend to loose them, and thus, they (the Democrat-Haves) will seek to replace these lost supporters; and as we have explained, they may look to open immigration from the economically disadvantaged countries.

D. Another way would be to piece together all the disparate groups of society which harbor various niche policies by contributing government money to their causes thereby attracting their support.

H. And taking this approach would surely cost dearly. As such, there is no appeasement of the fiscal appetite of the Democrats.

D. There is one further aspect of this that should be mentioned which is that these fragmented, special interest groups are usually those of society that want to control and regulate society using negative-knowledge plus force to make society more in line with its particular vision, or that is, its ideology. And to do so, it solicits the Haves to facilitate the implementation of its ideology.

H. But is it necessarily so that these special interest groups pursue the Democratic Party? I am sure that this is not the exclusive domain of the Left.

D. You are correct in that the Right also has under its wing some special interest groups; however, the Right does not pursue these groups en masse, by design, and as a political strategy to the extent the Left does; and this is because at its core the Republican Party is still the party of the principles of the Have-Nots and it attracts its voters through allowing the unrestrained production of knowledge through the adherence to the Dictums of the Have-Nots, particularly 1, 3, 5, & 7.

H. But at times, the Republicans give me pause to believe in this statement that they are the home of the principles of the Have-Nots.

D. Yes, I understand your doubts because when the Republican Party comes into the possession of the reins of government by controlling Congress and the Presidency, they become subject to the enticement of Dictum 5, the Lord Acton Principle, and hence, can become corrupted by the power of the situation which guides them into the province of becoming members of the Haves, the very party against which they frequently rail and criticize when they are not in total control.

H. Yes, that is right; and history has seen this very situation several times whereby the Have-Nots become corrupted themselves and jump ship to go over to the class of the Haves! And when they did so, they were scolded accordingly by their own party and by the voters in the next election.

D. There is one more salient characteristic that needs to be noted when the Have-Nots become corrupted by Dictum 5: they also move Left toward accruing greater control, and as such, the party in its entirety moves each time a little bit to the Left; and so when the Right gains control of the government, it moves Left much to the chagrin of many on the Have-Not-Right. Such is the power of Dictum 5.

H. Here's another question: do the Democrat Leftist-Haves honor the military? Do they think the military is important for their nation over which they rule? It seems that they are always trying to make the military less effective in times of peace.

D. A very interesting question.

H. They are constantly trying to cut the budget of the military and degrade it, yet history has shown us that the Haves have started almost every war (but not the revolutions which were many times started by the Have-Nots) throughout the last 5,000 years. Further, to make the situation more confusing, some Leftist-Have-Nations build up their military as if they were preparing for war and then there are nations, such as ours, whereby the military expenditures are cut when the Leftist-Haves get in power.

D. There are two reasons. The main reason that they will cut the military expenditures is because there is the lure of additional budgetary leeway that could be delegated to their constituent fringe Have-Not groups that receive largesse that make up the party to a significant degree.

H. That makes some sense.

D. The Haves know they should have a military, but at the same time they do not trust the military soldiers because the military personnel for the most part come from the class of the Have-Nots which the Haves look down upon because they are inferior and basically bad people, as per Leftist-Have-Dictum 3.

H. Schizophrenia! How do they overcome themselves? It is almost comical.

D. Easy. Throughout history, the Haves inserted commissioned officers to run the armies and navies. These officers were appointed by the Haves to whom they held their obligation to be loyal and from whom they received their commission to be an officer. This has been the situation throughout history. It didn't work perfectly as there have been rebellions whereby the military turns on the royal class, but it worked for the most part.

H. Even today? Even during modern times? It seems these days most of the officers are of the Have-Not class.

D. True, but nowadays, the Haves have replaced their emphasis on commissioned officers being loyal to the Haves to depending on compliance officers that make up much of the military today on whom the Haves rely (and have relied upon in the past also) to keep the military ideologically pure so that the Left can depend on their allegiance to the royal governmental Have-class.

H. Oh, yes, it is true. The Soviet Leftist-Haves had the party political officer embedded within all segments of the military, and it is becoming the case here in America. The Democrats upon gaining possession of the military and other institutions as well, such as education, insert their ideological compliance officers. I know that our alma mater, here, now has hundreds of compliance officers loyal to the ideals and ideology of the Leftist-Haves.

D. The Haves throughout history have always embedded their informants and the ideological pure within the military class as they have always needed the military to maintain power and pursue their priorities of that which is good for them, Dictum 1. Further, the Leftist-Haves in society in general have even induced the Have-Nots by incentives to report on others when something is said or done that is incongruous to the objective of the Leftist-Haves.

H. You mentioned that there is a second reason why the Haves tend to deprecate and depreciate the military.

D. The Leftist-Haves feel there should be no more need of a military as of the Treaty of Westphalia of 1648 which has become an ideology. As you know, the treaty was a major steppingstone in defining countries. First of all, it ended a long and devastating war that included most of the countries of Western Europe. It ended the war between the Catholics and Protestants, for the most part, as it recognized that the Protestants were to be present permanently in Europe. But the treaty did more than that: it defined borders of countries, and it got all the signatories to recognize and honor, at least briefly, these borders.

H. It was a turning point and milestone of European history.

D. And it was good for the Haves: it expanded, defined, and insured their respective territories. Then over the centuries, Westphalia became an ideology. At this point, let's remember that an ideology is the description of how other people should live and in this case this is what the purpose of the treaty was in that it was to define how each respective group of people, otherwise known as a nation, should be left to deal with its own individual internal problems. In other words each territory should be its own sovereign nation.

H. But there have been hundreds of wars since that treaty!

D. True. However, the treaty converted wars from religious to nationalistic only, by and large. Christianity usually was no longer a concern which would, by itself, generate wars.

H. Excuse me, but I hate to be a skeptic, but it doesn't seem to be a huge improvement.

D. Your point is well taken, but nevertheless, kings and queens now defend their countries and nations for the sake of themselves and other nations as well; and as we go into modern times, this applies to the presidents of nations also, as they have now been duly elected. Leaders of nations presently instead of doing that which is good for themselves will be more nationalistic and do that which is good for their nation as they see it. And one of the things that resulted from Westphalia is that the Haves will defend this ideology that the concept of a nation needs to be defended. This means that leaders will not only defend their particular nation but nations throughout the world which adhere to their proper ideology.

H. Some examples of this would help.

D. In this century, there are several examples of the Leftist-Haves defending their ideology of nationalism. JFK invaded Vietnam to stop the encroachment by other nations of communist orientation; LBJ continued that defending of the ideological encroachment; before that Woodrow Wilson defended the ideology of European nations by joining into World War I; FDR did the same in World

War II; Truman in Korea. They didn't need to enter the war except for no other reason then to defend the concept of nationality as each nation has its own nationalistic ideological sovereignty and this ideology originated at the Treaty of Westphalia.

H. OK, I can see that they would readily enter those wars because they can have the Have-Nots do their fighting, so it's no problem for them. It is that the Haves are all important and that the Haves are the state; again as you pointed out the expression by Louis XIV. After all, the Haves equal societal good.

D. Thus, to save the good of Westphalia and its ideology, the Haves look to implement it into the world by defending the nations of similar ideology as per the examples you just mentioned and others whereby the U.S. went to defend other nations because of the ideology of nationalism as derived from the Treaty. The ideology that is derived from this treaty is only to direct a nation's military resources for self-defense, or wage war for the benefit of another nation whose ideology is deemed to be worthy of defense if under direct attack from another nation. But this ideology does not permit conquest of others for the purpose of colonization. It is only for the purpose of defense of one's own nation or other nations with similar ideology which are deemed worthy of protection. The objective of a purposeful intentional conquest of another nation still lives with the seven Dictums of the Haves.

H. Oh, by the way, do you have a definition of these Globalists of which I recently have become aware. Their purpose seems to be that of consultants to the governments of the world.

D. Globalists are Super-Haves.

H. What are these?

D. The globalists are as you said: they are the world's Uber Consultants; they want to be the Philosopher Kings as Plato indicated in *The Republic.* These Super-Haves believe that because of their superior intelligence, power, and accomplishments, they are the world's anointed ones to guide the policies that the world governments should follow. They will be the Rightly-Guided Philosopher Kings that Plato explained that the world would need in order to prosper and profit efficiently.

H. Professor, to change the subject a little bit, have you ever gotten into an argument with a Leftist-Have? You can't argue with them, can you? Why do you suppose that is?

D. It is because of Dictums 3 & 6!

H. Okay, Dictum 3 is that the Left looks at the other person and thinks that the other is inherently bad and is ill-natured.

D. That's right, and because of that, even though you might say something that is good, has a good point, and has a rationality and logic to it, it'll be of no service for you because the Leftist will spot something that is bad about what you say, about your nature; it even may not have anything to do with what you're talking about. But because your nature is bad, everything you say must be bad, and therefore, the Leftist cannot ascent to your ideas, to your logic, or to your reasoning. If there is good reason within your argument or your point, the Leftist will just ignore it, and change the subject in order to avoid speaking about any of the good points that you would bring forth.

H. And Dictum 6?

D. Dictum 6, which is that the end justifies the means, suggests that control is the end desire of the Leftist. If debate cannot bring about the end that the Leftist seeks, then the logical arguments that a conservative might bring forth are to be avoided. Therefore, when conservatives speak before the gatherings of many, the Left will seek out these orators and shut them down per force typically by shouting and other such disruptions.

H. Wow!

D. As such, for the Leftist, the political end desires are of paramount importance and any ethical cooperative means or objectives are not important. It is not the goodness that is generated that is important; it is the control that is needed in order to effectuate the equality and equity of the Have-Not classes. Everybody must be equal in all ways.

H. 1984!

D. Yes.

H. So Professor, in conclusion, I would like to suggest that we come up with a succinct definition for the political Left and Right.

D. Sure. This would be the Have-Dictum 7: the Leftist is an individual who seeks freedom for oneself while seeking control of others to accrue further benefit to oneself and to society; and the conservative Right is a person who seeks freedom for all and for each to pursue goodness (Have-Not Dictum 7).

H. Is there a chance to put this definition into an equation as we have done with other antecedent concepts?

D. Yes, as we know, the Sacrifice equals the Reward, and hence, the Sacrifice for the Conservative Right person is composed of Risk, Knowledge, Knowledge of Cooperative Efficiency (if more than one person is involved), Time, Effort, and Material if it is a product; and if it is a service, then it is sans material. Thus, we may say that the Sacrifice for the Conservative Person (CP) is:

$$R_{(\%)}(K_{(byte\text{-}ergs)} + C_{(Cooperative\ Knowledge\ of\ Efficiency\ in\ byte\text{-}ergs)})T_{(sec)}E_{(ergs)}M_{(mass)}$$

And for the Leftist person (LP) we will need to add control; and as such,

$$(R_{(\%)})(K_{(byte\text{-}ergs)} + C_{(Cooperative\ Knowledge\ of\ Efficiency\ in\ byte\text{-}ergs)} + (\text{-}Negative\ Knowledge)))T_{(sec)}(E_{(ergs)} + (\text{-}Negative\ Effort_{(ergs)}))M_{(mass)})$$

And as we noted previously, freedom is represented by the creation and effectuation of knowledge and this is noted by a knowledge base; motivation is the comparison of the two sides of the equation; cooperation is the combining of the equations when multiple individuals are striving together by the C variable; competition and differentiation would be the change in the product of the sacrifice and reward sides of the equation over a period of time as the product of the equation either converges or diverges represented by vector analysis and noted as $\|v\|$. Thus,

$$LP = \frac{dt\|v}{(Convergence\text{-}Divergence)}\|Sacrifice = (R_{(\%)})(K_{(byte\text{-}ergs)} + (C_{(Cooperative\ Knowledge\ of\ Efficiency\ in\ byte\text{-}ergs)}) + (\text{-}Negative\ Knowledge)))T_{(sec)}(E_{(ergs)} + (\text{-}Negative\ Effort_{(ergs)}))M_{(mass)} : Rwd_{(The\ Good)} = (R_{(\%)}K_{(byte\text{-}ergs)}T_{(sec)}E_{(ergs)}M_{(mass)})$$

And the Conservative Right Proponent (CP)

$$CP = dt||v_{(Convergent\text{-}Divergent)}||Sacrifice = (R_{(\%)}(K_{(byte\text{-}ergs)}{}^{+C}(Cooperate\ Knowledge\ of\ Efficiency\ in\ byte\text{-}ergs)^T{}_{(sec)}{}^E{}_{(ergs)}{}^M{}_{(mass)}) : Rwd_{(The\ Good)} = (R_{(\%)}{}^K{}_{(byte\text{-}ergs)}{}^T{}_{(sec)}{}^E{}_{(ergs)}{}^M{}_{(mass)})$$

H. Excellent!

D. And, of course, you remember at the beginning of this conversation, we discussed the definitions of the various political ideologies?

H. Yes.

D. These ideologies all are the various iterations of the placement of control by the Haves upon the goods and services generated by the Have-Nots. No matter which ideology the political party employs, the controlling Leftist-Haves, due to their Dictums, historically have never relinquished their hold on this wealth produced by the Have-Not slaves except when forced by a revolution, and as such, we dare say, will never do so in the future.

Chapter 11: Goodness, Profit, & Aesthetics

------●○◇○●------

H. One final topic: in this and in previous interviews, we have spoken about goodness, especially when speaking of ethics. We noted that ethics is the appropriate dispensation of respect, that we respect others in order to cooperate to produce goods and services, and we produce goods and services to bring ourselves up away from misery.

D. Yes.

H. But I don't think we have adequately defined goodness. We've just said that we produce to bring ourselves up away from misery, but I suppose that we have not sufficiently defined goodness. We've just said that it brings ourselves up away from misery, but really, it doesn't let us know the essence of that which is good. It really seems to me that it is necessary to give more substance to the essence of goodness other than it to be the negative of something. So, what do you suppose is the nature of goodness or the nature of that which is good.

D. Goodness is that which allows life to prosper; or in other words, goodness is that which profits.

H. What? That sounds rather mercantilist! Sounds like life is trying to run a business. But I remember that we touched upon this in my previous book, *The Philosophical Equations of Economics*.

D. Goodness is the reward that we get from our sacrifices.

H. Therefore, our sacrifices equal our rewards which are equal to goodness, and so is equal to risk, time, knowledge, and effort that we use in our sacrifices which we do because of Dictum 1.

D. And when a sacrifice is successful in producing a reward, that life entity profits in that it receives goodness. Each time it receives goodness from its own sacrifices, it profits by its sacrifice. A commercial company is no different. Each time it receives a reward from its sacrifices which produces its products or services which it cooperatively exchanges by money or barter, it does so because of the expected goodness it will receive as predicted by Dictum 1. Thus, we may deduce that the rewards are generally good (but not 100% good due to the risk involved in life). Therefore, the company receives goodness from its sacrifice, overall (but is sometimes thwarted by the risk which is endemic in every transaction), and ergo, a company will profit from the received goodness. Therefore, profits, including company profits, are good in general.

H. Contrary to the opinion of some, I might add sarcastically.

D. In fact, the general purpose of life is to profit! Evolution, which is a word we should use to mean the probable involvement of the divine creator, (I say this because of my informal probability calculations indicate that genetic mutation alone cannot produce the complications as manifested by life entities) infused life with the will to be adherent to Dictum 1; and so life's basic and first overall objective is to do that which is good for it which is to profit from its sacrifices; and the more we are successful at creating goodness, not only for ourselves but our families, our society, and other life throughout the world, the more life produces profit. And as per your first opus, *The Nature of Aesthetics*, we may conclude that the more profit the life entities generate, the more the sacrifices are aesthetic.

H. Yes, aesthetics is the farthest and the most preponderant direction that evolution has taken any niche of life. Aesthetics is the farthest that evolution has produced, relative to any particular niche; and so, any entity that increases its production of goodness and profit, the more it is aesthetic and thereby beautiful. Examples of beautiful natures would be the highest forms of the animal kingdom such as whales, dolphins, tigers, lions, and horses. They are beautiful because they are examples of the farthest nature has gone in producing these examples of life niche-species. The human brain is an aesthetic marvel as it is the farthest evolution has taken intelligence. But aesthetics extends also to the inanimate world, such as, looking up on a clear night sky and seeing the Milky Way. When we do so, we are struck with the sense of beauty because our aesthetic sense allows us to recognize that the same forces and material of the wondrous stars are that which provides us with the production of Earth which allows us to live, survive, understand, learn, and prosper.

D. Well said. The more and to the greater extent that we produce goodness, the more we follow the path of that which is aesthetic which is the general purpose of life.

H. I noticed that you use the word "general" in the phrase "general purpose of life." Is there a specific purpose of life?

D. There is. The specific purpose is that life is to pass along knowledge.

H. Really? Interesting!

D. The greatest aesthetic inspiration that we may experience is to pass along our knowledge. Evolution has inspired us to follow this Dictum that all life should pass along knowledge. And so it is: we enjoy teaching, creating knowledge, and passing along information and knowledge to others. Evolution knows that this is an absolute need for the species to continue. As such, all the advanced life forms, such as mammals, teach their young as much as possible so as to survive in a risk-laden world.

H. It's true. All advanced species (especially our species) teach their progeny. But interestingly, you said "all life" not just advanced life entities such as mammals. Why did you mention this?

D. I said that because all life does reproduce and with it comes genetic knowledge that is passed along to the next generation. We all have this notion within us to reproduce. Evolution knows that it should not leave us the choice to only our cognitive portion of the brain.

D. Evolution doesn't want to leave the importance of passing on knowledge to others to only the cognitive portion of the brain, because we can tend to be very selfish. So, evolution instills in the genetics of the species the will to reproduce. This will to reproduce is actually a priority which is a piece of knowledge. As such, all life entities have the drive and inspiration to reproduce. And reproduction is the passing along of the genetic knowledge to create another life entity. But it is more than creating a life entity: it is the creation of another life entity with our particular knowledge stored inside the new entity, and in that, it becomes a high priority. And this passing along of knowledge, whether it be genetic or from the cognitive portion of the brain, is very important to us.

H. Therefore, teaching becomes an aesthetic thing to do.

D. And because of its ultimate importance, it becomes beautifully aesthetic. The passing of knowledge is the furthest and greatest expression of aesthetics; and the more the knowledge has importance, the more it becomes aesthetic.

H. Professor, thank you very much for your time and insight. I look forward to seeing you soon again.

D. Always a pleasure and do certainly stop by again.

H. I certainly will.

Milton Keynes UK
Ingram Content Group UK Ltd.
UKHW021117180124
436244UK00008B/81